He Wasn't Man Enough For Me

2

By

Autumn

Erica is doing everything in her power to destroy Khan's life and everyone in it. She will stop at nothing to get vengeance for her broken heart. Erica feels her actions are justified. What is she willing to do to get even with the man who destroyed her life?

Alani thought she was happy in her relationship with Rich, but now she's not so sure it's what she really wants. His career is starting to flourish and the groupies are flocking. Will he continue to brush them off and remain true to Alani?

Bam is in a fucked up head space because of Rock and the loss of their son. Will Rock's actions push her over the edge, considering her unstable mental state? Or will the new man in her life help her heal the demons that haunt her?

Khanna and Dae'Sean are finally at a good place in their relationship after she found out what happened between him and Brooke. But with new secrets surfacing, will their happiness last?

Kane's return has Megan feeling a certain type of way. As much a she wants to hate him, she can't. He has always had a way of pulling her back even when she tries to stay away. Kane does whatever it takes to get back into Megan's good graces, but is it too late to mend her broken heart?

Follow the family on a roller coaster of love, sex, lies, betrayal, and deception. Will they be strong enough to prevail or will their enemies bring them to their knees?

Find out between the pages of *He Wasn't Man Enough for Me 2*.

Chapter 1

Khan

I pulled up to Mama Angeline's house with my piece out, fearing the worst. When I made it to the front door I heard Alani let out a blood curdling scream. I burst into the house and followed her muffled screams. In all my years of life, there was nothing that could have prepared me for the sight that lay before me.

Khanna stood there looking like a deer in headlights. Alani was in the corner of Karizma's nursery rocking her mother, Angeline, back and forth in her arms. She was covered in blood and La'La was crying.

"Did you call somebody?" I asked Khanna.

She shook her head, yes, still looking shocked. I guess she wasn't able to respond with words.

Mama Angeline is the sweetest woman in the world. My mind couldn't grasp that somebody would want to hurt her. She had always been a nice lady, but I was determined to find out who attempted to end her life. The subtle rise and fall of her chest let me know she was alive.

I moved closer to Alani in an attempt to console her. Just as I was about to touch her shoulder she jumped back.

"Don't fucking touch me Khan; this is all your fucking fault! Everything you touch turns from sugar to shit. Now my Mama dying and my fucking baby is gone!" she yelled in my direction.

It was then that I realized that the crib and entire house were empty and baby free. The realization hit me like a ton of bricks. *Somebody had come and taken my fucking kids!* The fact that somebody had enough balls to come and touch my family let me know that this was personal. Even if it wasn't, I would have made it that way.

I didn't know who could hate me enough to mess with my kids. Karizma and KJ were my life and whoever snatched them was going to pay with their life. The moment they took them, they signed their own death certificates.

"Get the fuck out Khan! I hate you! I rue the day I even met you, you stupid black bastard!" La'La screamed with tears decorating her beautiful face.

I could never let her know that her words were like a dagger through my heart. There was nothing more for me to do but turn and stalk toward the door.

I bumped into Rich on my way out.

"What's going on?" he asked me with worry etched on his face.

I just shook my head and continued to walk down the stairs and out the house. He would find out on his own, when he walked into the lion's den.

I sat in a chair on the front porch and waited forever for the ambulance to make their appearance. I know La'La told me to leave, but what kind of nigga would I be if I actually left when she needed me. She might be mad at a nigga right now about some shit that was out of my hands, but looking back she will appreciate that I was still here, despite her snapping on my ass. Now all I can do is play the waiting game and hope that Mama Angeline makes it through this.

Chapter 2

Kane

It felt good as hell to be back at home with my old lady, after being gone for nearly two decades. I had been out of the loop for the majority of my kids' lives and I wanted nothing more than to make up for all the time I'd lost. If only Megan would let me. She's been giving me a hard time when I ask for her to set up a meeting between us.

I've heard through the grapevine that Khan is the man to see around town. I would have picked a different profession for my only son, but I couldn't complain too much considering the fact that I haven't been in his life. Contrary to popular belief, I have always wanted what was best for my kids even from a distance.

I still made sure that Megan's pockets were laced; which is why they were able to live so comfortably without her ever having to work. Where they lacked in having my presence, I attempted to make up for it in money. I used to wish I could've turned back the hands of time, but seeing as though that can't happen, I played the cards that had been dealt.

Back in the day when Khan and Khanna were kids, I started creeping with this chick named Giana Milano. She was the daughter of Giovanni Milano, head of the Milano crime family. Megan is, and always has been, under the impression that the Milano crime family was after me because I fucked their money up. It's true they were after me, just not for that reason.

I had been fucking his 18-year-old daughter on the sneak tip. After a while when she got tired of creeping with me, she gave me an ultimatum. She told me that I needed to come clean with Megan and her father; saying she was tired of living in the shadows. She also said that if I didn't that she was going to leave me.

I told her that I needed more time. Shit, I wasn't trying to fuck up my home front; I knew what side my bread was buttered on. But its only one thing better than pussy and that's new pussy. Megan's shit is bomb, but Giana's was out of this world; she was young and had never been touched.

She was always walking around the Milano estate with tight ass clothes on and my lil man wanted a taste of what she had to offer. Even though I knew the daughter of such a powerful man was off limits. Curiosity got the best of me. Giana had a body that was stacked in all the right places. She was 5'9 with pretty, light olive-colored skin, long wavy hair, and high, defined cheekbones.

She didn't have much ass but her rack made up for what she lacked. Her legs were so long they seemed like they went on for days. She has a mole under her bottom lip and a small nose ring in her nose. Giana's lips were thin and her big doe like eyes drove me crazy.

Now I'm not saying that she was prettier than Megan, but they were just two different types of beautiful. Gianna ended up telling her father about what was going on between us and he put a hit out on me. Giana thought she was doing something good, but Giovanni sheltered her and she didn't realize that she'd opened up a whole new can of worms.

I would have been dead if she hadn't overheard her father discussing my execution. Once Giana got wind of what her father had planned for me, she packed up her shit and hipped me to what was going on. I packed up my shit as well and fed Megan a half-truth story about what went down.

We already had passports, so that was one last thing that we had to worry about. After that we hopped on a plane going from country to country until we felt like shit had died down. We finally settled down in Guyana. I reached out to Megan and told her to assist me in faking my death. I attended my own funeral and I felt like shit watching my kids from a distance. Khanna was bawling her eyes out and I wanted nothing more than to comfort her.

The way Megan was crying you would have thought I died for real, but I guess she was mourning the death of our relationship. She knew deep down that things would never be the same for us. My biggest regret of all is being such a selfish ass nigga. Megan didn't deserve any of the shit she had to go through because of me.

I used to reach out to her every now and again to check on the kids, but once she got wind that I married Giana, all that ceased. The pictures she used to send to my P.O. box stopped and all communication between us ceased. That didn't stop me from making sure her and my kids were straight financially.

After a few years of being married, Giana got pregnant. She hated having a baby without her family being there; so behind my back, she called her father and told him where we were. She told him that she was in labor and wanted him to be there for the birth of his first and only grandchild.

I walk into the hospital thinking that everything was good until I see a couple of his henchmen standing outside her door. Thinking that they found our location, I go to our home to pack up some stuff and move her to a different hospital. When I got back to the hospital, I was informed that she and the baby died while she was giving birth.

I was never allowed to view her or my baby girl's body. The hospital said that her father had claimed the bodies. I hopped on a plane and moved out to Trinidad, until I finally came home to Megan.

Once I was back in the states, I wanted nothing more than to live a prosperous life with my children and the only woman that holds the key to my heart.

Chapter 3

Bam

I rolled over in my king sized bed with my 1200 thread count Egyptian cotton sheets clutched around my naked frame. For the first time in a long time, I woke up with a smile covering my entire face. I felt so liberated. I had to duck off for a little bit to get my mind right. I was officially back to being 'Bam that just doesn't care.'

The first thing I needed to do was handle my hygiene. So I made my way to the master bathroom to brush my teeth and wash my face. Turning on my shower, I waited until it got to the appropriate temperature before I stepped in. After thirty minutes and scrubbing my body four times, I concluded my shower.

I liked to air dry, so instead of drying off I just placed a robe around my body and walked downstairs to the kitchen. I decided to make up an omelet with turkey bacon. On the side, I had mixed fruit and orange juice.

When I finished my breakfast, I cleaned up the small mess I'd made. Just as I was going back upstairs to find an outfit for the day, I was interrupted by the ringing of my door bell. I opened the door to find the guy that was with Rich at the hospital the day Alani got shot.

"Yo Ma, I need for you to go put on some clothes and come with me" he replied all in one breath.

I looked at him with a stank face. Then I pulled my robe tighter, remembering that I was next to naked. At the same time, I was taking in his appearance; this tall glass of chocolate milk was straight up intoxicating, or was it his Hugo Boss cologne? Either way I was lost in his appearance and I wanted him. That didn't mean I was going anywhere with somebody that I didn't know from a can of beans.

I guess he noticed the mixture of lust and hesitation on my face because he said "Look, I know you don't know me, but I'm only here as a favor for Rich. He said something is up with Alani."

That was all it took. I didn't even bother to respond to him, I just took off for the stairs and my bedroom. I grabbed a pair of Seven jeans that were laying on the chaise, threw on a tank top from my dresser, grabbed a black pair of air force ones, my keys, and purse then I made my way out the door; but not before I grabbed Smith and Wesson.

"Let's be out playboy," I told the guy whose name I had yet to catch.

I know how to handle myself in the face of adversity, which led me to getting in the car with a perfect stranger. Once he said something was up with La'La, I felt bad for the hiatus that I had taken from my loved ones; but I needed some time for myself. I hopped into his Infinity and melted into the leather seats. His car smelled like black ice air freshener.

I didn't speak but I noticed how we were riding in the direction of the hospital. The closer we got to the hospital, the antsier I got to the point that I couldn't stop fidgeting in my seat. If I lost my sister, I'll slide right back into that dark place.

When we pulled up to the hospital, I jumped out the car without waiting for him to park. I ran to the front desk and asked the lady for Alani's room.

Popping her gum and flicking her long nails, she said with an attitude, "I don't have an Alani Thomas."

Willing myself to calm down, I asked, "Well do you have an Alani Clarke?" My patience was wearing thin.

"Nope." she said still popping that damn gum.

My patience had officially worn out; I grabbed her by her scrub top.

"Bitch, I know my sister is here, so you're going to tell me which room she is in; now!" I growled with spittle flying on her face.

"I don't have an Alani Clarke, but I do have an Angeline Clark. She's in room 2103," she said in one breath. Hearing that, my heart sank to my feet.

What could be wrong with my mama? She isn't my real mother, but blood couldn't make us any thicker.

"Thank you. Now was that so hard?" I replied letting her go before stalking toward the elevators.

I'm not a mean person, people just bring out the worst in me. Right then, my main and only concern was finding out what's wrong with my mama.

Chapter 4

Rock

I woke up feeling like shit the day after Sophie burst up in the crib. Bam had every intention of killing us when she broke into the house that I share with Margo, while we were having sex. It was like something snapped in her, but she just walked out the door leaving us there.

Margo didn't know who Bam was. She knew of her, but she couldn't point her out while walking down the street and I liked to keep it that way. That was until Margo took her monkey ass to the hospital demanding answers to questions she wasn't mentally prepared to hear.

Bam came into the room and shot Margo in the foot, then tried to stab her in the stomach. I tackled her and she had a faraway look in her eyes. Bam started mumbling incoherently while I continued to calm her down.

She then stabbed me in my hand, got away, and grabbed another gun out of her boot. Just as she was about to pull the trigger, she dropped the gun and walked out.

I had to drive Margo and her fucked up foot to the hospital with one bum hand.

After the doctors patched us up, we were sent to an ultrasound room to wait for them to come and check the baby. While I waited, I admired Margo's entire frame; 5'11 with long legs and the complexion of peanut butter. She is a model and a self-proclaimed make-up guru. She kept her hair in a short cut that framed her face perfectly.

I started fucking with Margo one night at a club called "The Cabin," a little hole in the wall joint in Virginia Beach. She stood out in a crowd full of ratchet bitches, looking like she didn't belong.

I was kicking it with some of the little niggas under me, refusing to go home to Bam. She had gone crazy on a nigga earlier.

***

I had placed my outfit for the day on the bed and went to take a shower. When I came out, I put my boxers on and my nuts started itching out of nowhere.

Shortly after, my dick started burning. I hurriedly took my boxers off to see my whole dick and balls covered in fire ants.

"SOPHIE!" I screamed out to her while trying to brush them off of me.

She came in the room wearing a mug saying, "What Rocky?" like she hadn't done anything.

"HELP ME GET THIS SHIT OFF OF ME BITCH! THE FUCK IS WRONG WITH YOU?!" I questioned her ready to snatch her fucking head off.

"Well you should have never ate the rest of that strawberry cheese cake La'La made for me and the baby," she said with a straight face like the shit really made sense to her. "Now go hop your dumb ass back in the shower to rinse em off and I'll rub you down with some calamine lotion," she added like everything was immediately all good then walked out the room.

***

Later that night after checking on each trap, I went to the club. I needed to be good and fucked up before going home to the spawn of Satan. Meanwhile, Margo stood at the bar looking out of place and irritated so I approached her.

"What you doing in here shorty? This place doesn't seem like it's your type of stomping grounds," I said to her.

"Well I was in the area to meet up with a client, but she canceled at the last minute," she replied while looking me up and down. I could see it in her eyes that she was pleased with what she saw.

I had never been a cocky nigga, but I was damn sure confident.

"Well, how about I take you to a place that's a little classier," I suggested.

"You don't strike me as the type to know a classy place," she said snottily. But it didn't matter because I knew that sooner or later I was going to be knee deep in her walls. I could tell by the curiosity in her eyes that she was intrigued by a nigga.

"Well why don't you follow me and find out," I told her.

"I caught an Uber here so I don't have a ride," she said holding her head down.

"Don't ever hold your head down while you're with me. Now let's go," I told her standing up and straightening my clothes.

"Um, excuse me, but I don't know you," she said with her bougie demeanor resurfacing.

"But you want to, so finish up your drink and I'll be in the car waiting," I replied.

Just like I thought she would, she said, "I don't even know which one is yours."

"Oh you'll know," I threw over my shoulder and walked out.

She met me at my car and the rest is history. I was going to take her to Chic Lounge, but decided against it. I didn't need Envy running her mouth to Sophie's loony ass. We ended up walking the strip that night. Long story short I had her face down, ass up on the beach and she's been my bitch ever since.

***

I sat in the hospital looking at her bruised and scratched up face. "What Josiah?" she asked feeling my gaze on the side of her face.

"My bad shorty, I didn't mean for any of this shit to happen," I told her sincerely.

"Who is she, Rock?" Margo asked calling my nickname. She never calls me that name, so now I know she's really mad.

"Nobody," was the one-word response I offered her.

"Why did she say that we stole her son's name? How did she know where we live? Did you fuck her in our house? Why was she trying to kill us? Were you and her in a relationship?" Margo rattled off question after question and I didn't know which one of them to answer first.

In all actuality, I didn't want to answer any of them. I knew I'd lied to both Bam and Margo, but at the same time, I didn't want to throw either of them under the bus at the expense of the other's feelings. I never talk down about one of my bitches to another. That's some straight hoe shit and there isn't an ounce of bitch in my blood.

So I sat stone faced while Margo stared me down waiting for an answer to her many questions and I gave her none.

"You know what Rock, just get the heck out! Me and MY SON will be just fine without you!" she screamed.

She was seconds away from pissing me off, putting emphasis on the words 'My Son' like I wasn't the one knocking that pussy out the frame to put that lil nigga up in her.

"Go be with that bitch and her son. You claim to be a real nigga, but can't even be man enough to answer a few, might I add, very logical questions. I don't want to see your face if you can't be honest with me. Until then, we are done," she stated with finality.

I continued to remain seated, but refused to utter a word.

"Why are you still here? Don't you have a bitch and a bastard baby to go see about?"

I refused to dignify her comments with a response, but she was really pushing it.

"Go check on them because you are not wanted here. Make sure your bitch and your son of a bitch are fine, you no good…" that was the last thing she got out before I was on her ass choking the life out of her.

I hated to be putting my hands on her while she was carrying my seed, but she pushed me to the limit.

"I'm not leaving until I know my seed is good so sit back and shut the fuck up; and the next time you speak ill of her or my son will be the last time you speak any words for that matter. Got that?" I sneered in her face with spittle flying.

She just shook her head, yes. I could smell the fear oozing from her pores. Margo had never seen this side of me before. She didn't know Rock, she only knew Josiah and they were two totally different people.

I was always sweet, loving, and caring when dealing with her, but my son was still a sore spot for me. Bam was mad because she was under the impression I was trying to replace Lil Rocky by making me and Margo's son a Jr., but that couldn't be further from the truth.

Margo, since she didn't know about Bam or Lil Rocky, insisted on him being a Jr. Eventually, I just stopped arguing with her and just allowed her to think that he was going to be a Jr. When it came time to deliver him, that would be a totally different story.

I already have a Jr. and just because Lil Rocky didn't make it; that doesn't mean I'll have another baby using his name. As far as I'm concerned he's still here.

Chapter 5

Alani

I was sitting in the hospital while my mother struggled for her life and the experience was beyond the worst feeling in the world. Not to mention my daughter, Karizma, was missing along with her brother KJ, Khan and Brooke's son who is only older than Karizma by a couple of weeks. Some lunatic broke into my mother's house and snatched the kids. She got shot trying to protect the children.

The only person who could hate me enough to want to kidnap my daughter was Brooke's extra envious ass; Khan's side chick turned baby moms. If we weren't holding her in a warehouse and her son wasn't missing as well, I would have sworn up and down that it was her dizzy ass.

I knew it couldn't be her so my mind was racing. My mother was stable, but unresponsive, due to her being in a coma. I hadn't said a word since got there. Khan and Rich had both been trying to get a reaction out of me, only for me to stare blankly into space while clutching my leading lady's hand tightly.

I definitely was not in the mood to talk and be attempting to hold a full blown conversation with someone who didn't feel my pain. When I looked into their eyes, all I saw was sympathy that I didn't want or need. Even Megan felt sorry for me when she came up here to make her cameo appearance.

I hated when I felt like it was me against the world and that I didn't have anybody in my corner. Just as I was about to let my thoughts consume me, in struts Bam. She looked good even though she was dressed down indicating that she rushed over here. She had an undeniable glow to her that seemed to brighten up the dark and gloomy room.

I felt slightly better knowing that she had come out on top of her own personal problems. She is also the only one who I feel is here in sincerity. My mother adopted Sophie when we both were kids. We've been tight since the sandbox and I didn't see anything changing that.

"Ma," Bam whispered.

She pulled a chair up to the opposite side of the bed. She buried her head in our mother's chest and hugged her neck, carefully as not to disturb the monitors.

When she pulled back, her eyes were moist, but she never let a tear fall. We made eye contact and no words were needed. Bam and I kissed our mama's forehead simultaneously and walked out. I left strict orders with the nurse and doctor that no one was allowed in my mother's room and to call me if anything changed about her condition.

We were dressed in all black and rode out with murder on our minds. It was time to bring my babies home.

Chapter 6

Erica

I had been up since six o'clock with a crying and fussy Karizma. KJ was in his bouncer eating while I had Karizma in my arms. She was finally calming down and slowly drifting off to sleep. KJ was so advanced for him to only be slightly older than his sister. He held his own bottle and self-soothed while I tended to Kay. Being a mother of two is hard, but I'm determined to be the best mother I can be.

Once both of them were asleep I laid them inside of their cribs, turned on the baby monitors, and went to take a nap myself. If only their father would have come by and offered me some assistance. It's not like I laid down and made those babies by myself. I wasn't going to force Khan to be in the lives of his children though.

I could take care of my kids right by my lonesome. Just as I was about to fall into a peaceful slumber, there was a knock on the door of my townhouse. I continued to lay in bed hoping they would go away. They were persistent and didn't let up; alternating between ringing the doorbell and knocking on my door like the fucking police. Reluctantly I got up not wanting KJ and Karizma to wake up.

I checked on my kids first, making sure they weren't up. They were still sound asleep and I just hoped they stayed that way so that mommy could get some rest. I rushed to the door ready to lay out whoever deemed it necessary to bang on my fucking door.

"WHAT THE FUCK DO YOU WANT!?! DO YOU HAVE ANY IDEA OF HOW EARLY IT IS!?!" I screamed as soon as I flung the door open. When I realized it was my sister Arianna my anger intensified.

"What are you doing here Arianna?" I asked folding my arms across my chest.

"So I can't come and check on my little sister?" she smirked pushing her way into my home.

"Well just come right on in," I replied sarcastically following behind her.

"You never come by to see any of us and we've been worried about you. None of us have seen you in nearly a year," she said.

If I didn't know any better, I would have actually thought she cared, but I'm no fool. None of then gave a damn about me, never have and probably never will.

"If it was up to me it would have been another year," I stated unbothered.

"Oh Erica! You had a baby and didn't tell anybody?" Arianna's nosey ass asked me with mock excitement looking at the toys and bouncer on the floor.

"None of your damn business Arianna! You've checked on me as you can see I'm fine, so now you can get the hell out of my damn house!" I guess I screamed a little too loud because both kids started crying through the baby monitor.

"Get the fuck out, Ari. I want you gone out of my house and my life when I come back," I seethed before making my way up the stairs.

When I made it to their room I picked my cry baby Karizma up first. KJ had already stopped crying and was playing with his rattle.

"OMG Erica! You had twins?" Ari asked picking up KJ and kissing his chubby cheeks.

"Since you must know yes I did," I stated irritated with her entire presence.

"Oh shit, I'm an auntie now. What are their names?" she asked.

"Khan Junior and Karizma," I replied refusing to give out more information than she needed to know.

"I would love to watch them any time you need a break. You know you should really bring them to the house to see Mama I'm sure it would make her feel better," she said gushing over my kids.

"I'll think about it," was my only reply.

After calming Kay-Kay down I placed her back inside of her crib.

"Erica you look like you're exhausted. I don't mind sitting here to watch them while you rest for a little bit," she offered.

I didn't want this bitch in my house any longer, but I know that it was the only way that I would have gotten any sleep.

Against my better judgment I allowed her to stay. As soon as my head touched the pillow I was out like a light. I knew she was up to something, but I figured I would find out soon enough what her ulterior motive was.

Chapter 7

Arianna

Allow me to introduce myself and give you a smidgen of our backstory. I'm Arianna May, Erica's older sister. We come from a one parent household, well kind of, my father died shortly after my second birthday of cancer. So it was just me and my mother. When I was three years old, my mother met Eric, Erica's father, and that's when things started to change for me.

My mother was so stuck up his ass she started to pay less and less attention to me. Shortly after he moved in, she became pregnant with Erica. Eric's creepy ass used to watch me shower or creep into my room at night and watch me sleep. Good thing is he never touched me just watched or take pictures.

One day I finally decided to tell my mother that I didn't like him and what he does to me and she whooped my ass. I never told her anything else about him after that. When Erica was born, it got better and her father actually treated me like his daughter. But I still felt like something was off with him.

One day my mama went to take Erica to the doctor for a checkup and left me home with him. I watched him sit at the coffee table in the living room and sniff coke. He did it right in front of me, like I wasn't even there. I didn't utter a word about it.

A few months later he and my mother got into an argument and he started packing his shit.

I heard my mother tell him, "Pack up your daughter's shit too, she going right with your ass. I'm not raising this damn demon child alone. You're a demon so I know she is because she got demon blood in her."

He grabbed their shit and left. I could have jumped for joy when that door slammed shut. It's not that I didn't love my sister, I was just anxious for things between me and my mother to go back to normal. For years I didn't see Erica. I'm not exactly sure if my mother was seeing her either. My mother met another man when I was about ten and he treated me way better than Eric; we were like one big happy family.

Then my mother got pregnant with my little brother Major. Not too long after his birth, Erica moved back in with us. Eric had conned his way into the heart of some wealthy woman and said he didn't want her anymore, as if she was just a piece of property. When she came back she acted weird. At first she wouldn't talk to anybody. I was pissed because in our three-bedroom house, even though I was the eldest I ended up sharing a room with my kid brother while E got her own room.

She was acting like she was too good to live with us on some days, while other's she just stared off into space. Sometimes she would bang her head on the wall until it bled. I don't know what Eric did to her, but that coke snorting bastard fucked my baby sister's head up something terrible. My mother turned a complete blind eye to what was going on with E.

When we were in school Erica was a complete rebel. She was always fighting and getting suspended. She remained defiant all through of our adolescent and teenage years. Her father got her an apartment when she turned 18. After that, we didn't see much of her.

When I turned twenty-one the man that we all thought was God sent fell sick, only for us to find out that he had HIV. My mother got checked just to find out that she had it too.

Erica landed a good job as a massage therapist at a high end full service salon. Her father kept her bank account laced, I guess to make up for his absence in her adult life, but she doesn't even attempt to lend a hand towards my mother's hospital bills or expensive ass medications.

I love my sister still, but I know that bitch needs help. Major is still just a kid so he can't really help and his bitch ass dirty dick daddy, Big Major, died of full blown AIDS. So instead of branching out and spreading my wings, I'm still at home taking care of my mom and little brother.

*****

While I was watching my niece and nephew I searched their faces for some family resemblance. For us to all have different fathers we all look smack like my mother. I saw none of our Spanish heritage in those kids. They both have a chocolaty smooth complexion. Maybe they take after their father. I just wanted to know who was dumb enough to knock Erica up. She must not have had an episode while dealing with him.

I fed them both and laid them down to nap. Then I got up to start my search. Before Erica went to take a nap, she told me to stay out of the room at the end of the hall, so that was the first room I intended to check. When I went to turn the knob, it was locked; I picked it.

Rummaging through the desk and file cabinets all I found was papers from a shrink. I didn't need anybody to tell me she was crazy I been hip. I grabbed a few of the papers with her diagnosis listed on them. Before leaving, I made sure everything was back into its original place and locked the door behind me.

I didn't see any place she could hide things so I just sat down in defeat. I guess I could have just sat and chilled until my sister woke up. Right when I sat down on the love seat I saw her phone on the end table. Eager to find out some tea, I picked it up and hit the home button. I could have jumped for joy when I realized that she didn't have a password on it.

The first place I checked was her photo gallery. Scrolling through all I seen was a bunch of pictures of some tall dark skinned guy with dreads. He didn't look like he was paying attention in any of them. Like he didn't even know they were being taken. There were also some pictures of him with other women. As I kept scrolling through, I found some pictures with him and their kids.

It was then I assumed that he was Khan, my sister's baby daddy. But then I saw pictures of the kids with two different women. They were at the park having picnics and things like that; none of the pictures were of Erica. I sent all the pictures to my phone and deleted the evidence. I scrolled through her contacts until I found Khan. I knew he was the one in the pictures because she had a contact photo saved.

I put his number into my phone and put Erica's phone back exactly how I found it. The timing couldn't have been more perfect, because Erica came right down the stairs.

"Thank you so much sis I needed that. Having two kids with two different sleeping patterns was starting to take a toll on me, but I manage," she told me yawning.

"It's no problem girly, I got chu anytime," I replied then added, "Well I'm going to get on out of here, I'll talk to you later. Don't be a stranger."

"I won't. I'm going to try to come by mommy's house one day this week to check y'all out, and so she can see the kids," she said.

"Please do. I think Mama would love to know she has grandchildren," I told her before giving her a hug and leaving.

I couldn't get out of there fast enough. I need to get home and call this Khan character. I just can't seem to shake this nagging feeling that those kids did not come from my sister.

Chapter 8

Rich

Blake and I had been scouring the city for leads on who could have taken the kids and tried to off La'La's mom dukes.

"Yo, my nigga, what's up with Bam?" Blake asked me.

"What you mean, 'what's up with her?'" I asked him not feeling the direction this conversation was headed.

"I'm trying to get with that." he told me flatly.

"I mean, that's La'La's best friend; they're practically sisters. But what I can say is tread at your own risk, she's a woman scorned," I warned him.

"That ain't shit I can't handle," he said rubbing his hands together like Birdman.

"I'm telling you now, you better not go near her unless you're serious. Bam and Alani don't play, especially if somebody fucks with the other. They're not typical females, my shorty and her best friend are straight cutthroat, and they're as thorough as they come. Bring the hardest nigga you know around and they'll bring him to his knees screaming like a bitch," I told him trying to put him on game.

"I got this my nigga, don't worry about me," he said looking out the window.

"Say no more." I replied.

"Yo, when we getting back in the studio?" Blake asked me.

"Are you serious my nigga?" I asked him just to get some clarity.

"Dead ass," he stated with no sense of humor.

"My fucking daughter is missing nigga! I could give less than a fuck about the fucking studio right now!" I snapped on his ass.

"My bad Dog, we gone find your shorty. I was just wondering when we were going to get back to this money?" he said obviously not hearing shit I said.

"Not a minute before I find my seed," I told him agitated.

"No doubt my dude," he replied.

Sometimes Blake had me wanting to fuck him up about the shit that came out his mouth. The last thing on my mind was the fucking studio, when Karizma and her brother were missing. On top of that, the same person tried to body Alani's OG.

We had been driving around for hours and haven't gotten anywhere, so I put the word out to one of my old homies that it's a price on the head of the culprit. I needed to get my little girl home as urgent as yesterday.

Chapter 9

Khan

I don't know how we let Bam and La'La slip through the cracks like that. There was no telling where they were or what they had up their sleeves. Leaving the hospital, I headed to my condo to take a shower. My body was dying to take a nap, but I couldn't sleep knowing anything could be happening to my kids.

After cleansing my body, I went to the warehouse where Brooke was being held. I had to let her know that our son was missing.

When I made it to the room where she was being held, I opened the door and said, "Get dressed," then walked away. Shortly after, she joined me at the table in the conference room.

"What the fuck do you want Khan? If you came here to kill me, you could have been did that. I already told ya'll, I didn't shoot La'La and I don't know who did. Just get it over with. I've already made peace with myself and God for all of my wrongdoings. The only thing that I ask is that you make sure my son is well taken care of and when he gets older let him know that his mother loved him and tried to do right by him," she said rambling.

"Brooke, shut the fuck up! If I came here to kill you, you would've been dead!" I snapped to shut her up.

"What do you want then?" she asked me.

I had to take a deep breath before continuing, this is not information that you ever want to deliver.

"Somebody got KJ."

WHAP! She slapped the shit out of me as soon as the words left my mouth.

The last thing I ever wanted to have to tell my baby mama was that I failed to protect my kids. Brooke started raining blow after blow on my face and chest.

"How could you let somebody take my baby Khan?" she sobbed into my chest once I restrained her.

"Let's go." I told her once she had calmed down although she was still distraught. I don't think anybody would be mad about me removing her from the warehouse at a time like this. She might have done a lot of fucked up shit in her life, but I knew she genuinely loved KJ.

I took her to one of my apartments to clean up, while I called a meeting at my mother's house. It was time to bring my fucking kids home.

*****

Brooke, Khanna, and I made it to my mother's house before everybody else. Using my key to open the door, I let us in. As soon as I flipped on the lights in the dark house, I wanted to walk right back out. My mother was butt ass naked in a standing 69 position with some nigga.

"What the fuck is this?" I boomed startling them.

"Oh shit, get it mama!" Brooke exclaimed laughing.

"Eww, I think I just might lose my lunch," Khanna said covering her eyes.

"Oh shit!" my Mom yelled. "I didn't think ya'll would be here so soon."

"Put some fucking clothes on!" I yelled.

I really wasn't trying to hold a conversation with my mama while she and some random nigga were standing in their naked glory.

"Bruh, if you know what's good for you, you would get the fuck up out of my mama's house!" I snapped once they were fully dressed.

"Khan, wait I have something to tell you," my mother said.

"You can tell me whatever you want once this nigga gets out," I stated matter-of-factly.

"Lil nigga you got one more time to pop slick out the side of your neck," this random nigga said getting buck.

"What the fuck you gone do about it bitch ass nigga?" I asked moving closer towards him.

Next thing I know that nigga hit me. Then it was on and popping we were going blow for blow fucking up the house in the process.

"What the fuck is going on in here?" La'La asked walking into the house with Bam in tow, followed by Rich, Blake, and Rock.

Without even knowing what was going on Rock jumped in and bum rushed the nigga.

"Stop this shit!" my mama yelled but her words fell on deaf ears.

WHAP! WHAP! WHAP! Bam hit all three of us with the butt of her gun.

"Now let's get down to business," she added while stepping over us.

The three of us all got off the floor and simultaneously brushed off and straightened out our clothes.

Heading to my mother's oversized dining room we all sat at the table. I took my rightful place at the head of the table. Alani sat at the other end across from me with Bam to her right and Rich to her left. Blake sat beside Rich, my mother sat beside Bam, Khanna sat beside my mother, and random dude sat across from them. I had Rock on my right and Brooke on my left.

I took a moment before speaking to take in this table full of dysfunction. Brooke looked out of place and sad; Alani looked mad at the world, as she should be; Bam and Rock both shared evil glances; Khanna's face held a blank stare; and my mother and this random nigga exchanged flirty glances.

"Before I start my nigga you gotta raise up out of here. This is a matter of family," I sneered to the nigga that was fucking my mama.

He kept sitting there like I wasn't talking to his ass.

"My nigga, I'm trying to tell you that this ain't what you want, so fuck off," I added pulling out my Ruger and sitting it on the table.

"Khan put that shit up," my mama said.

"I will once this nigga leaves," I firmly stated.

"Boy, I think you might want to listen to your mama," this nigga had the nerve to say.

"Fuck you just say to me fuck boy?" I asked him pointing my nine straight at his dome.

"Put that shit down Khan, now. I told your dumb ass that I had something to tell you. Now sit ya'll dumb asses down so we can find my babies."

I sat down, but refused to put my strap up. "Okay, so obviously I know everybody is wondering who this is," mama said pointed at him. "Well this is Kane," she then waited to gage our reactions. Confused expressions covered the faces of everybody in attendance.

"Kane is Khan and Khanna's father," she added.

All of our mouths formed the letter "O" as the astonishment settled in. This nigga is supposed to be dead.

Chapter 10

Khanna

To hear that my father was alive gave me mixed emotions. The sadness that I once felt for not having a father was quickly replaced with anger for him abandoning us; his family, his own flesh and blood. You have to be a different type of coward to just up and leave your whole family high and dry, regardless of the reason.

A little girl's father is supposed to be her first love. That is the man that is supposed to show her how she is supposed to be treated. Looking at my brother's face I can only wonder what's going through his head. He's too calm right now. I never saw him raise his gun, but I didn't miss it going off. He had shot our "Father" in the arm; I do use the term father loosely.

Kane just sat there, ripped a piece of his shirt, wrapped it around the bullet wound, and never got up from the table. He just held his hand there to apply pressure to stop the bleeding. Nobody flinched and carried on like nothing mattered.

"Now back to the matter at hand," Khan continued.

"Somebody has my kids and I don't have the slightest clue as to who could have them. Not to mention they tried to kill La'La's moms. I've had my ear to the streets, but they're not saying anything. I have a quarter of a million on the head of the person responsible. Now what I won't do, is sit around idle while my kids are out there," Khan said while scanning the room.

Just as he was about to continue his phone rang. He rejected the call only for them to call back. Khan put his phone on vibrate, but his phone rang again sliding across the table.

"You might want to answer that it could be one of your hoes," Alani smirked at him.

They were constantly throwing shots at one another and I just thought it was the cutest thing ever. They need to just stop their shit and get back together.

You could see the reluctance on Khan's face as he reached for his phone.

He answered it, "Talk to me."

"Yo, who's this?"

"I'm listening."

I was getting irritated being able to only hear one side of their conversation. But seeing how his jaw clenched and the wave of seriousness that washed over his face I could tell it wasn't good news and the plot was about to thicken.

Chapter 11

Khan

The constant ringing of my phone was pissing me off. Nothing at that precise moment was more important than finding KJ and Karizma unscathed, but to humor Alani, not that this was a laughing matter, I answered it.

"Talk to me," I answered.

"Hello, may I speak to Khan?" a woman whose voice sounded unfamiliar asked.

"Yo, who's this?" I asked them.

"You don't know me, but my name is Arianna and I'm Erica's sister," she said.

"I'm listening," was my only reply.

My curiosity started to settle in. Why was Erica's sister calling me? I haven't fucked that bitch since before I proposed to Alani.

"I just want to ask you a few questions, I promise not to take up too much of your time," she said.

"Proceed," I told her, ready for her to get to the gist of her call.

"I would prefer to ask them in person. Is there anywhere that you would like to meet me?" she asked. I rattled off my mother's address to her then ended the call. If this bitch was on some good bullshit I wouldn't hesitate to put a bullet in her dome. So now we wait.

*****

A small knock on the door drew the attention of all of us. I opened the door for a woman who resembled Erica, only she was prettier.

"Hi," she shyly spoke. Now was not the time she needed to be shy. I could have been out looking for my seeds, but instead I was entertaining her ass.

Nobody spoke back, but they all gave her ass the mean mug of death.

"Khan, do you mind stepping out so we could speak privately?" Arianna asked me.

"Yes, bitch he minds!" La 'La snapped with much attitude.

Before this situation got out of hand I said, "Anything you have to say to me you can say in front of them, this is my family."

I led the way back to the dining room and everybody took their seats, but never took their eyes off of Arianna. I know they're wondering who the hell she is. "I know you are probably wondering why I called you; well it's about your kids," she said. But before she could say anything else Bam and Alani were on her ass standing right behind her chair with their guns cocked. Everybody else had simultaneously aimed their straps at her head, even Kane's pussy ass with his one good arm.

"OMG, what's going on?" Arianna cried seeing all these guns pointed in her face.

"What about my kids?" I asked her as calm as the ocean.

"Can you tell them to put their guns down first?" she asked shaking like a stripper.

Everybody lowered their guns except Bam and La'La, but that was to be expected with their thug asses.

"As I was saying," she continued "I went to visit my sister and saw the twins, but I never even knew anything about her being pregnant. I haven't seen her in over a year, but I went to her house to talk to her. My mother is really sick as she has been for years, but it has gotten worse and I have a hard time taking care of her and paying her medical bills.

"I went to Erica's house to see if she could pitch in a little bit. She tried to kick me out, but I wasn't having it. I watched them while she took a nap and I searched through her house. There were no family portraits or anything so I looked through her phone and saw that there were no pictures of her and the twins, only you, and them, or two other women," Arianna continued.

"Do these two women here just so happen to be the women in the pictures you seen?" I asked her while pointing at Alani and Brooke.

"Yes, actually they are I have the pictures right here in my phone," she said handing me her phone.

My temperature continuously rose with each scroll through her phone. This bitch had pictures of me and Shaunda, me and Alani, me and Brooke, me with both of my children, and pictures of all of them separately. My jaw involuntarily clenched just thinking about how long she could have been following us and nobody noticed. I never even realized she could possibly be a threat.

When I looked up from the phone Alani, Bam, and Khanna all had their weapons out and trained on Arianna. Brooke sat there giving her the death stare, probably because she didn't have a gun.

"Well how do we know that you didn't take our fucking kids and are here to collect the money my baby daddy and man have on the heads of the culprit for your sick mother?" La'La growled menacing into her ear.

"Money? What are ya'll talking about? I don't know anything about any money," Arianna said rattling off questions cowering in fear from the amount of guns in her face.

"Look, here's Erica's diary. I haven't read anything out of it, but I can guarantee it has something valuable in there. She has been keeping one since we were kids and she writes down everything," she all but frantically yelled while throwing the diary on the table.

I grabbed it and skimmed through the pages quickly. One page in particular caught my attention. This bitch wrote in grave detail how she singlehandedly wreaked havoc on my family. How could one bitch catch a team of thoroughbreds slipping to this magnitude?

To learn that this bitch had tried to kill my wife, my mother-in-law, and took my kids had me livid. It was now my turn to hold a gun to this bitch's head. "Where the fuck does she live?" I growled in her ear. "Are my kids with her?"

"The kids are at my mother's house," she trembled.

"Let's go," I responded by snatching her up.

I was just that much closer to bringing my kids home.

Chapter 12

Erica

Against my better judgment, I left my kids with my mother so that I could do more reconnaissance on Khan and his crew. I just couldn't find any of them, so I headed to my mother's house to pick the kids up. As I turned on her street, I noticed the front of her house barricaded with cars. Just when I found a spot a few houses down I spotted Khan coming out the house with my kids.

To say I was livid would be an understatement. Once again here he is trying to take what's rightfully mine away from me. My children have been my world since I got them, they're the only thing that kept me sane. I don't even know how he knew where my mother lived let alone that our kids were there.

My confusion cleared as soon as I saw my bitch of a sister, Arianna, walk out of the house behind them. I watched Khan hand her some money before they all pulled off.

I crouched down in my seat to ensure that they didn't see me while driving past. My sister is going to pay with her life for the shit she just did.

*****

I put getting my kids back on the back burner, only so I could figure out Arianna's routine. I watched my mama's house long enough to know that Arianna no longer lived there. With the money my baby daddy gave, her she bought a condo in downtown Norfolk in some high rise. I had my hair in a ponytail and a snapback pulled low over my head. For them to be luxury condos I got in rather easily. They didn't have a doorman.

When I made it to her condo, I picked the lock and made myself at home. I knew she was gonna be gone for a while because she had taken my mama to her doctor's appointment. My stomach had been killing me all day, so my first stop was the bathroom to take a shit. After reliving myself, I watched reruns of *Love and Hip Hop New York* with my feet kicked up on her coffee table.

I don't know how much money Khan gave her, but she had this bitch laid out. That only added fuel to the already burning flame Khan ignited in me. Then she wants to throw a monkey wrench in my fucking plans, all for a few bands.

"What are you doing in here Erica?" Arianna asked walking in.

This bitch had her hand on her hip like she had an attitude or something, when I should've been the one mad; I mean my kids did get taken. Before responding I looked her up and down. This hoe was rocking a Dolce & Gabbana rose printed chiffon shirt, with some red capris, and white and silver Tory Burch sandals.

This nigga had really come in and upgraded her ass.

"Um, Hello? Earth to Erica. I was talking to you. I asked you what the fuck you were doing in my house?" she said with a little more bass in her voice than I would have liked.

"You know why I'm here," I said doing my best Marshawn Lynch impersonation, standing up, and slowly walking up on her.

"No, I don't, if I did I wouldn't have asked you," she snapped again.

"You sucked the devil's dick for a little bit of money," I responded.

"Erica, right now you're just babbling like an idiot. Please get to your reasoning for breaking into my place, so that I can then show you to the door," she countered snootily.

"You aided Khan in taking my kids from me!" I blurted out.

"Oh, so that's what this is about. Erica those were not your kids, and now they are with their parents where they belong," she had the audacity to say.

"Yes, they are my children and they belong with me," I snapped on her ass.

"No, you're just a crazy bitch that took somebody's kids and tried to claim them as her own."

That was the benediction. I charged her into the table and it broke on impact. We rolled around on the floor for a few going blow for blow before I got the upper hand and and pinned her down. Who would have known that Arianna's ass had a lil bit of hands?

I proceeded to bang her head into the hardwood floors.

"THOSE ARE MY KIDS, BITCH! DON'T YOU EVER SAY THAT SHIT AGAIN! THEY'RE MINE! THEY'RE MINE!" I yelled.

I must have been doing some type of damage because, her movements eventually started to slow. When she stopped moving completely, I checked her pulse to ensure that she was indeed still breathing.

Then I dragged her to the dining room and tied her to one of the chairs. I hope she didn't think I was done with her ass.

Chapter 13

Bam

After finding the kids in one piece and getting the hood doctor to check them out, I decided to take my ass home. This day has been very eventful. Since I left my car at home and rode with Blake, I got him to take me back home. La'La was loving on my niece and I didn't want to break up their happy moment.

I was low key feeling some type of way about seeing them with their kids. I was supposed to be able to come home and hug my son, but that would never happen.

"Thank you," I told Blake once he pulled up in front of my house.

"No problem lil lady," he responded with a panty wetting smile.

I knew I had to hurry up and remove myself from his presence, so I rushed towards my door.

As soon as I got it open, he called out, "Aye ma, can I use your bathroom right quick?" he asked.

I guess sensing my reluctance to let him in my house he added, "I gotta pee bad as shit."

Throwing caution to the wind, I said fuck it and told him to come on.

I gave him directions to the downstairs bathroom, told him to show himself out, and to lock the door behind him. My bed was calling my name and I didn't want to wait any longer to answer it.

Walking into my room, I stripped and threw my clothes in the hamper.

I let the plush carpet caress my feet while slowly walking toward the master bathroom. I cut on the shower and when it was the right temperature, I stepped in and allowed my whole head to be submerged under the water. I immediately felt the stress of the day melt from my soul.

Feeling a cool breeze and another person in the bathroom caused my eyes to pop open. There was Blake in all of his naked, magnificent, glory standing before me. His dick was hanging down his thigh like a third leg. Before I could respond with words, he was in the shower with me.

He never said a word only grabbed my shampoo and started washing my hair. Even if I wanted him to stop I couldn't formulate the words, because of the orgasm he was giving me by massaging my scalp. I stood there and let him wash and condition my hair relishing in feeling.

After he completed the task of cleansing my hair, he washed my entire body; even my ass and my vajayjay. That nigga cleaned me from the rooter to the tooter. I was floating on cloud nine.

Once he finished me, he cleaned his body with some of Rock's Dove for Men body wash that I had yet to get rid of. Stepping out, he dried both of us off, and led the way to my bed. *No need for clothes,* I thought. He still hadn't said a word.

I hopped my lil ass in my four poster bed and waited for him to join me. My kitty was jumping in anticipation of what was to come, or so I thought. He climbed into bed behind me, cut on the radio, and grabbed me from behind with his dick resting comfortably on my ass.

This nigga never even tried to make a move on me; he just held me all night. I wanted to push his ass off of me, hop on his dick, and take him on the ride of his life. But instead I enjoyed the feel of his strong muscular arms holding me and I eventually dosed. *How could I be mad at a nigga for just wanted to lay with me, no pussy involved?* For the first time, in a long time, I slept carefree with a smile on my face.

Chapter 14

Kane

After getting my grandkids squared away with their parents, Megan sat with me while the hood doctor patched me up. The hood doctor was a cat that went to medical school, finished, and got his degree, but didn't feel right working a nine to five. So he made his dough helping people out of the same hoods he grew up in. Khan paid this nigga a pretty penny to have him on call whenever somebody needed him.

"Sooo, that went well," Megan said sarcastically.

"That lil nigga shot me," growled in pain as the doctor stitched me up.

"Well what did you expect? I mean the first strike was when he walked in on you fucking his mama, the only parent he's ever known. The second strike was you fought him. The benediction was when he learned that you were his quote unquote father, the man who abandoned his family. Really, how can you blame him?" she said, pissing me off further.

"Fuck that, that lil nigga going to respect me whether he wants to or not. He came from my nut sack!" I snapped.

"Whatever Kane I'm not about argue with you. You are just going to have to win both of your kids over; really all three of us, because I'm not too convinced either."

I know I've made some not so savory decisions in my time, but I thought about my family every day that I was gone. Granted, I did love Gianna too, but it was a different from how I felt about my Megan.

She's been down for a nigga through the shine and the struggle. I knew that the road back into her heart and the hearts of Khan and Khanna was going to take some time, but I was more than willing to foot the bill.

"I know that I fucked up, but I'm willing to work the rest of my life showing ya'll how much you mean to me, but not until after I show Khan that I'm not to be fucked with though. Now, bend that fat ass over so we can finish what he interrupted."

Fuck the pain in my arm, I was ready to be balls deep in Megan's walls.

Chapter 15

Rock

"Baby, you gotta breathe easy" I said coaching Margo through her Braxton Hicks contractions.

I failed once and was no longer taking any chances when it came down my kid's lives.

"But it hurts so bad," she cried out.

"Everything will be okay, just breathe and try to walk." I continued to console Margo until the pain she was feeling subsided.

After ensuring that she was okay, I headed out. I haven't been fucking with her like that since that bullshit she said to me at the hospital. I didn't give a fuck if I was being petty or not. This bitch wasn't about to talk to me any kind of way.

After a slight battle of emotions, I came to the conclusion that I would go and check on Bam. It was near impossible to miss the look of despair on her face once our close friends and family were reunited with their children. I picked her up some extra magazines for her favorite gun and hot wings before making my way to the house we used to share.

Bam could eat hot wings at any time of the day, they were her favorite food. You can't buy a bitch like Bam flowers or even candy. My bitch is a straight thoroughbred and there is not a day that goes by that I don't miss her. She has always been the realist nigga on my team.

If only I could turn back the hands of time, it would be Bam, Lil Rocky, and me; no Margo. Don't get me wrong, I intended on loving my seed to the death of me, but my heart wasn't in our relationship like hers was. My heart was and always had been with Sophie. Pulling up to her crib, I backed into the drive way; you never know if you'll have to make a quick escape.

I was tempted to knock on the door, but opted to open it with my key. She never did change the locks on me.

"Sophie!" I yelled once I walked in. She didn't respond, but I could hear her voice coming from the kitchen. I walked in to find her midget ass butt naked sprawled out on the island in the kitchen getting her pussy eaten by Blake.

"WHAT THE FUCK IS THIS!" my voice boomed off the walls. Sophie jumped up and tried to cover herself while Blake looked me dead in my eyes smirking, with my bitch's pussy dripping off of his chin.

I lost it, I never wanted another nigga to be able to say he knew what my bitch tasted or felt like. I hit that nigga smooth in his jaw, but before I could follow up I noticed that nigga was naked too. I'm not about to fight no nigga with his fucking nuts out.

I looked Bam in her eyes, but was unable to read her.

"You slut ass bitch, Fuck you," I snapped. I picked up the shit I had gotten her that had fallen to the floor during the struggle and threw it in her direction.

I stormed out of the house only for her to follow me, "Rocky wait! We didn't fuck or anything!" she screamed behind me. "Carry yo' dumb ass in the fucking house Sophie! You got your titties out and pussy juice running down your fucking legs," I snapped noticing she neglected to put any clothes on.

She looked like she wanted to protest, but the look on my face made her turn around and retreat back into the house. Getting in my whip, I noticed his car parked in front of her house. That nigga was going to have to see me about touching what he should have been known was off limits to him.

I did feel a little better knowing that she ran behind me to check me out instead of staying behind to check on that nigga. I needed to release some pent up frustration; I went to Margo so she could suck and fuck all my stress away.

Chapter 16

Alani

Ever since I got my baby girl home, I want nothing more than to love on her.

"Hey my Kay-Baby, Mama missed you," I cooed while kissing her face all over. Words could not describe how lost I was without my baby girl. Karizma was my life.

I still couldn't enjoy my daughter being home like I wanted to because the bitch that took her was still at large. Just like Khan to have a bitch in the cut that nobody knew about. I was clueless about this Erica bitch, until I saw the pictures in her mother's house. It was the ditzy, bimbo bitch from Diamond's shop that was throwing me shade when we went there for my birthday.

After feeding my daughter, I laid her down for a nap. My baby had gotten fat since I had last laid eyes on her. At least that hoe wasn't abusing my baby. She was going to get handled either way, but I would cut her misery short for taking care of my baby.

I left Karizma's room and grabbed my phone to make a phone call.

"Hello, you've reached Diamond the slayologist, how may I assist you?" Diamond's extra ass answered the phone.

"Yes, I need to be slayed by the slayologist," I responded playing into her pettiness.

"Girl, you know I will always make time for you," she said laughing.

"Yeah I know, but that's not what I'm calling for right now," I told her changing my tone.

Sensing the switch in my demeanor she became concerned, "What's the tea boo? Spill it."

"What can you tell me about Erica?" I asked her.

"Erica, that works for me?" she asked.

"Yeah her," I responded.

"Girl, that's one of my best employees. Why you wanna know about her?" she asked me.

Usually I don't just sit around pillow talking about my family's affairs, but I fucks with Diamond, plus I knew that I had to tell her something in order for her to come up off of some information.

"That bitch shot my mother and kidnapped my kids," I blurted out.

"Well in that case, she no longer works at Heavenly Touch; you have to have a heavenly attitude to work in my place of business. I don't know much about her, she usually keeps to herself, but I will give you the address that I have on file for her."

"That would be greatly appreciated," I told her.

Diamond rattled off the address then asked me, "Should I go ahead and buy my black dress."

"You better believe it," I responded before ending the call.

I called up Bam and Khanna and as expected, they were ready for whatever. Reluctantly, I shot a call to Brooke. Shit, I know if somebody had taken my baby I would want to be in on the get back, so who was I to deny her of the privilege of a little revenge?

*****

We piled into a rented Toyota Corolla that couldn't be traced back to us. The tension inside of the car was so thick that it could be cut with a machete. Instead of saying something to cure the awkwardness, I cut on the radio.

The only on my mind was getting my hands on the bitch that tried to kill my mother, who was awake and out of a coma.

Khan always had bitches coming out of the woodworks and going crazy over his ass, but I'm the one that always drew the short end of the stick. I needed to rid myself of him ASAP.

As soon as I bury this bitch Erica, I'm making it my business to go see Mrs. Fitz and get his dirty dick ass served with divorce papers.

Pulling into her neighborhood, the street was practically deserted which was a plus in my book. I spotted her house and parked down the street. We sat there and waited for the light that was on upstairs to go off. A half an hour later, it did and it was game time.

"Alright ladies, it's show time," I said taking the safety off my gun.

I handed my .357 to Brooke because she is the only one who wasn't strapped already.

"Game time," I quoted and we all simultaneously exited the car.

We were dressed in black and green camo; no need for a ski mask because this bitch wouldn't be living long.

I already had the layout of her house, so I knew exactly where to go. Leading the way around the back of the house, I checked her side door. It was open. She sure was making shit extra easy for me. Making our way through the house, the first room we checked was the room the light had just gone off in. After years in the game, I still was not prepared for the sight before me.

Arianna was hog tied in the corner and Erica was standing over her sodomizing her with a big black dildo.

"Well, look who joined the party?" Erica said menacingly.

She took a step toward me with the shit and blood covered dildo still in her hand. Arianna looked as if she would pass out at any moment from the pain.

"Bitch, take another step and it will be your last," Khanna sneered in a venom laced voice.

Who knew my lil protégé grew some balls recently? Everybody had their straps out pointed in Erica's direction.

"No need to get hostile. Three out of five of us all have the same man in common," she laughed.

"Bitch, you made this a hostile situation when you touched my fucking son!" Brooke snapped "Now, come on willingly before I have to forcibly remove you."

To say I was impressed by my lil goon squad would be an understatement, but now is not the time to gloat.

"So, I finally get to meet the women behind the man who can't seem to keep his shit together. I must say, I didn't foresee us meeting under these circumstances, but hey you know what they say…"

Before she could articulate any further, Bam shot her in the temple with a bean bag round. She hit the floor with a loud thud, knocked out cold. We all just looked at Bam and she looked at us shocked, like we were wrong

"What? She talks too much, but she'll live. When she wakes up she will just have one hell of a headache."

We shook our heads and pitched in on carrying her out of the house and taking her to the warehouse. I had to do a little convincing to get them to help me with Arianna.

"Hell naw man, that bitch is covered in shit! It feels like I might lose my lunch just from looking at her," Khanna complained.

I covered her with a sheet I found in the linen closet. "Okay, now help me put her in the car. I'll call the hood doctor to come and check her out once we get there."

Once we had them both squared away in the trunk, we pulled off into the night en route to the warehouse.

Chapter 17

Khan

La'La sent a mass text telling everybody to meet her at the warehouse. I noted that Brooke, Khanna, and Bam were conveniently left out, which led me to believe they were all together and up to no good. It's a damn shame that the women in my life get into more shit than the men do. After scooping up Rock, I headed in the direction of the warehouse.

I knew this couldn't be good especially since Alani had turned into as much of a hot head as Bam since she got shot.

When we pulled up, I only saw one unfamiliar car out front, I guess me and Rock were the last to show up.

After opening the door and meeting everybody in the conference room, I smiled. My family may have been what some would consider unconventional, but at the very least we knew how to stick together in times of need.

"Now that y'all have decided to make an appearance, let's get started," Alani said sarcastically.

Instead of responding, I mugged her then followed everybody. A smile stretched across my face. There was Erica, hog tied in the middle of the torture chamber naked; it made my dick hard.

"The hood doctor will be in shortly to care for Arianna. Since this bitch deemed it necessary to do what she did to her sister, I'm going to do the same to her," Alani sneered.

I stood back and watched while Bam, Khanna, Brooke, and their ring leader Alani all got dressed in something similar to a hazmat suit. Brooke pulled out the biggest dildo I've ever seen in my life. That shit was so big it was like something you would read about in one of those urban fiction books La'La be reading; not something you would see in real life.

"I was gonna lube it up for you, but seeing as how you didn't give your sister that choice... I'm not going to give you one" La'La said with a sinister pause. As she stalked closer to Erica with the dildo in her hand, Erica's eyes grew big as saucers and damn near bucked out of her head. She attempted to back away, but the restraints wouldn't allow it.

"Ya'll come hold this bitch still," La'La said to her minions and they followed suit. They held Erica still while La'La morphed into a demon and she abused her anally with the dildo. The rag in Erica's mouth came out and her screams filled the warehouse, bouncing off the walls.

When Alani was finally satisfied, they all stood up.

"Khan come hose this bitch off, she stinks," La'La said to me while taking off her suit. "I'm hungry, so we'll be back once I get some food in our systems. But don't think for a second I'm done with this hoe. For touching my family, she'll pay with her life," and with that they all walked out.

Chapter 18

Erica

I definitely underestimated these bitches. For them to even to get at me had me feeling some type of way. I almost fainted when they burst into the room like Rambo, but I couldn't let them see it. All I remembered was talking shit one moment and waking up in the warehouse next.

I was low-key mad that I didn't get to finish off Arianna. When I saw Alani walking towards me with a dildo even bigger than the one I used on my sister, I actually got scared. When she shoved it in me, I died and came back. It felt like my insides were being split in half. These girls showed me no mercy.

In that moment, I regretted everything that I had ever done to cause them any harm. By the time the torture was over, I had passed out from the pain. I wished they would just kill me, but it was only wishful thinking.

*****

My eyes popped open to Bam standing over me with the smelling salts that she'd just snapped under my nose. My entire body ached and my ass was on fire, but at the same time I was shivering from getting sprayed with a high powered water hose.

"Rise and shine hoe! I know you didn't think that death would come to you that easily, did you?" she laughed in my face, "Baby we're just getting started."

"Khan, Rock, come put this hoe on the lift," Bam said. I felt myself being suspended in the air, but I was too weak to do anything about it. My eyes closed and my head fell back, but they quickly snapped open when I felt my flesh being ripped from body. Each of the women took turns beating me with chains wrapped around their hands.

Each time I passed out, they would wake me back up and continue the torture. I didn't know how much more I could take before the blood loss ran its course.

"Glad that you could make it and be a part of the festivities," I heard what sounded like Alani's voice.

I willed myself to open eyes and saw Arianna. She looked like her regular self with the exception of the bruises around her neck and the two black eyes she was sporting courtesy of me.

I honestly can't even say that I feel bad about it. If she hadn't gone to Khan about any of this, I would still have my kids and I wouldn't be here. In my eyes, this was all her fault.

"Bitch, you got my fucking kids taken away from me! I'm gonna kill your dumb ass!" I screamed bucking in chains. Just as I was getting my life back on track, she just had to come in and fuck it up.

"Bitch those weren't your fucking kids. I don't think you're in any position to be making empty threats," she smirked at me only further fueling my anger.

"Yes, they were and you got them taken away from me!" I countered back. "You really are a stupid, delusional ass hoe," she smirked again purposely pushing my buttons.

"I'm not crazy and I was a good mother to both of my children," I snapped.

"Oh, so we're finally getting to the gist of what this is all about. Daddy, gave you too many at home, back alley abortions that shredded that uterus of yours? What? You thought I didn't know about that? You may have gotten pregnant, but you and I both know you never would have carried to term."

"You read my fucking journal? I'm going to fuck you up bitch!" I screamed trying to break free knowing that it wasn't going to happen.

"Okay, I hate to break up this little sibling rivalry, but I'm sick of breathing the same air as the person who attempted to murder me and my mother," Alani said.

I guess it's redemption time and it's time to pay for all of my past indiscretions. Instead of a hail of bullets hitting me, I was lowered to the ground.

"Rock, did you fire that bitch up already?" Alani asked him.

"Yeah sis, that muthafucka is hot and ready like a Little Caesar's pizza," he replied. I wondered what the hell they were talking about. My body was dragged through the building and my question was answered.

These niggas had a fucking incinerator in this bitch! I started kicking, screaming, and trying to get away. I knew it was impossible, but I had to at least shoot my shot.

Bam stomped on one of my legs breaking it instantly and pain shot through my entire body. I stopped moving and just let them do what they had to do. There was no sense trying to prolong the inevitable.

They picked me up and threw me inside, because I just let go and became dead weight. The flames quickly engulfed me. I smelled the disgusting stench of my own burning flesh. My skin melted off me and my body burned to a crisp. I was no longer.

This was my fate when all I really wanted was to live in paradise with my children.

Chapter 19

Khanna

Since all the people who threatened my family's lives were gone, I could rest easy. I had a doctor's appointment to find out the sex of my baby. Dae'Sean's ass was a no show so I was left to go to it alone. I didn't want to know the sex of my baby, so I told my doctor to put the ultrasounds in an envelope that I would be giving to Alani since she was the one who was throwing my gender reveal party. In fact, she was the only other person that knew I was pregnant besides Dae-Dae.

"Everything is looking good Ms. Thomas, but it does seem like you've been doing a lot of stressing and straining lately. I advise you to take it easy," my doctor told me.

"No problem, I was going through some things at first, but now everything is all good," I replied, knowing the past few months had been hectic.

"Good, per your request, I have the sonograms in this envelope for you. You can stop by the front desk to set your next appointment. Make sure to get plenty of rest."

I thanked my doctor, set my next appointment and left. I was going to lay into Dae-Dae ass for missing my appointment when he promised he would be there. I pulled up to my house and saw the mailman walking towards my mailbox.

"I'll take that from you," I said and thanked him.

I threw the mail on the couch to check later and went to go take a shower.

I couldn't move fast enough because re-runs of Empire and a pint of fried ice cream were calling my name. After showering, I moisturized my entire body; paying close attention to my stomach with cocoa butter to prevent stretch marks. I was trying to snap right back after dropping my load.

I threw on a cami and some yoga pants, grabbed my ice cream from the freezer, a spoon, and made my way to my Italian leather sectional. Grabbing my remote I went to Hulu and started Empire. I was cracking the fuck up at Lucious and Cookie. They still love each other, I just wished they would get it together; kind of like my brother and Alani.

I paused the show to use the bathroom and the mail caught my eye. I made a mental note to check it when I came back. After reliving myself and washing my hands I went back to the den and grabbed the mail before sitting down and making myself comfortable. Most of it was junk mail or bills that I had already paid, but one piece in particular caught my eye.

It was addressed to Dae'Sean, but it had come from the DNA Diagnostic Center. Curiosity got the best of me and I ripped it open. In big bold letters, clear as day it read:

In the case of Khan Thomas Junior, Dae'Sean Lassiter is 99.9% the father.

I flat out refused to read any further. The little boy whom I had grown to love as a nephew was my stepson. That shit didn't even sound right. He was a Jr., but the son of another man.

When I found out Brooke had slept with Dae-Dae, the possibility of him being the father never crossed my mind. There were some questions that needed to be answered, like how the hospital said Khan was a match when KJ was born? I was determined to get some answers and quick. I grabbed my Ugg boots, a light jacket, and was out the door.

Since all the bull shit had died down, Brooke had moved back into her old house; that was my first stop. Khan not being KJ's father would crush him.

I made the twenty minute drive to her house a five minute one. I hopped out the car not bothering to close the driver side door or turn off the ignition. I banged on her door and wasn't leaving until the bitch opened it. I had blocked her car in, so she wasn't going anywhere.

"Damn Khanna, you banging on my door like the fucking…" I didn't give her ass a chance to respond before I pounced on that ass.

"BITCH YOU HAD A BABY BY MY NIGGA THEN TRIED TO PIN IT ON MY BROTHER!" I screamed pounding her face in.

On the drive over, I actually sat back and thought about it. When she was in the hospital and KJ was having complications, Dae-Dae was there. I initially thought it was because he wanted to check on me while I was with Alani; that nigga was the one whose blood was used for KJ the whole time. He just must have not known for sure since Khan gave blood too and Brooke was a conniving bitch.

"Brooke, what the fuck you in here making all this damn noise for? Who was at the door?" I looked up and made eye contact with a shirtless Dae'Sean.

I got off of Brooke and charged his ass. I swung wildly hitting him in his face and chest scratching him.

"YOU NASTY DICK BASTARD! YOU HAD A BABY WITH THIS BITCH, AND YOU'RE STILL FUCKING HER! I HATE YOU MUTHAFUCKA!"

Brooke continued to lay on the floor in the same position I left her in. That bitch knew she didn't want no smoke with me. I always had to fight her battles while growing up. With as much shit as she used to talk, you would have thought she had hands.

Dae-Dae grabbed my arms attempting to calm me down.

"Chill the fuck out Khanna! I told you about putting your hands on me."

I looked at the nigga like he had grown five heads. He couldn't be serious? After what I had just found out this is what he was mad about? He better had hoped Khan showed him some mercy.

"Well congrats my nigga, you're the father!" I said.

I spit in his face and dropped the DNA results on the floor in front of him. I walked out the door with my head held high. I refuse to give them muthafuckas the satisfaction of seeing me cry, but as soon as I get home, I'll let it all out. There wasn't even anybody I could talk to about it, so I headed home to wallow in my own self-pity.

***

Brooke and Dae have been taking turns blowing up my phone. Dae'Sean has already stopped by the house, but I had already packed his shit and sat it outside and got my locks changed. I should have known he was a no good nigga, because I foot the bill for everything. Love has a way of blinding you and making you see past all the obvious signs until some shit goes down and God gives you no other choice than to open your eyes and see people for the snakes they really are.

The last time she called me, I just went ahead and answered it. I felt like the least I could do was listen to what the fuck she had to say. "What the fuck do you want?" I answered.

"I'm sorry Khanna. I know that our friendship has been a little strained lately, but I never meant for any of this to happen. When I found out that I was pregnant the possibility of Dae'Sean being the father never crossed my mind. Then when I had KJ, they told me his father needed to come and give blood because I wasn't a match. I got Khan to give blood, but then they told me he wasn't a match either. So that's when I called Dae'Sean. I never said anything because I was too dead set on destroying his relationship with La'La while solidifying my position in his life. But then, I felt like Dae-Dae had a right to know that he was the father of my son.

We've been sleeping together ever since, but he said that he wasn't going to tell you until he got the DNA results and found out for sure that KJ was his son. I told him when KJ was still in the hospital that Khan was the father. Ever since almost losing my life and KJ, I have been trying to become a better woman," she vented.

"Are you done?" I asked her.

The last thing I wanted to hear was her little sob story. Fucking my man not once, but twice isn't an accident, unless she tripped and fell on his dick, and I doubted that was even plausible.

"Yes, I'm so sorry," she pleaded.

"Well do you wanna know how you can make it up to me?" I asked her as soon a plan popped into my head.

"Yeah I'll do whatever."

"My gender reveal party is this weekend. Oh yeah I'm pregnant" I said with a slight laugh. "I want you to come, bring my baby daddy, and my nephew, oh I mean stepson, and you're going to tell Khan the truth about everything," I told her.

"Everything? Oh no, Khanna I can't do that. Khan will kill me," she responded sounding scared.

"You can and you will. You should have thought about what he might have done to you before you started popping that rotten peach you call a pussy for every Tom, Dick, and Harry. I'm starting to think you like being a side chick. You're the only bitch I know that has made a career out of sucking and fucking dick that's already spoken for," I matter-of-factly stated.

"Okay," was her only response before I disconnected the call with a smile on my face even though I was slowly dying on the inside.

This weekend was going to be so eventful and I couldn't wait. I had just gone from an expecting fiancé to a pregnant baby mama in a matter of less than twenty-four hours.

Chapter 20

Alani

I walked out of Mrs. Fitz's office with a smile plastered across my face. I had just got the news that Khan was being served with divorce papers. I was that much closer to washing my hands of his ass. He would be nothing more than a father to Karizma. Mrs. Fitz said that when he signed the papers that she could get the process expedited. Hopefully, that nigga made this process as painless as possible.

I had been neglecting Rich while dealing with all of my family problems, so I planned on making it up to him. I pulled some strings and got Envy and Adonis to set up a meeting with him and Blake to discuss a record deal, since they own a record label. I know that my baby has the skills to make this shit happen and I was just happy that I could do something special for him.

Since Karizma was with Megan and Kane and Rich was in a meeting, I stopped by Michael's to pick up some stuff for Khanna's gender reveal party. I rented out a reception hall to throw it in. I wanted to cater the food so I wouldn't have to worry about it or be pressed for time, but Khanna wanted me and Megan to cook instead. I asked her ass how Megan and I could cook when nobody it's a secret and nobody knows that she is with child.

She agreed with me, but I had to agree to make her a strawberry cheesecake to stop her pouting. After leaving Michael's, I stopped by Party City to get a couple more things and then I headed home, unloaded my car, and got settled in.

I called a couple vendors and sent down payments to the caterers and the reception hall. I planned on making the cake myself so there was no need to call a bakery. As soon as I finished I left to go pick up Karizma. I hate leaving my baby for any amount of time, especially since Erica's loony ass took her.

*****

The day of Khanna's gender reveal party came and I felt like a chicken with my head cut off. I made all the deserts the night before, so I was happy to have that out of the way. Rich, Blake, and Bam were all helping me decorate the reception hall. I had everything decorated in white and gold so that you wouldn't know off back what she was having.

I lied and told Megan and them I was throwing Rich and Blake a party for signing a record deal with Envy and Adonis, which was partially true. I was throwing them a party at CHIC, but it wasn't until after Khanna's event.

"Hang those balloons at each end of the desert table. Then repeat the same process on that table over there will the food will be," I told Rich.

"Has anybody heard anything from the caterers? I'm seconds away from putting my foot up somebody's ass!" I snapped.

People were due to start arriving in thirty minutes and the food still wasn't here yet. To say that I was ready to snap would be an understatement. Just as I was about to call the people they walked in.

"About fucking time! Place the food on the table in the far corner," I pointed in the general direction. Twenty minutes later everything was in place and I couldn't contain the smile the crept across my face. Everything came out gorgeous, even better than I pictured it; so good I had to pat myself on the back.

"Damn sis you, did the damn thing," Khanna said walking in.

Her outside appearance looked great with her form-fitting white maxi dress with all gold accessories picked out to match the decorations of the reception hall. But the look on her face, under the smile, told a different story. Something was wrong with her and I was determined to find out what it was before the night was over.

"Thank you boo, I try," I responded. I let her skate off while I stood by the door to greet everybody. Once I made a mental head count of everybody and that the main people were there, I headed to the podium up front and grabbed the microphone.

"Thank you for all coming out, we really appreciate it. If Khanna would come up front, we have something to tell ya'll," I said scanning the crowd.

When Khanna came up, I could see the confusion on some faces when their eyes fell on her protruding belly that seemed to have popped up overnight.

"Hey y'all, again thank you for coming. This is a celebration party, but not for what ya'll think. I'm expecting and this is my gender reveal party!" Khanna squealed. I could tell she was excited about becoming a mommy.

"What the fuck you mean expecting, Khanna" Khan snapped making his way towards us with a menacing scowl on his face.

"Like I was fucking and I got pregnant," Khanna said with her nose turned up.

This is not how I was expecting them to react. Kane grabbed Khan before he could come all the way up to the podium.

"Not now son," Kane said to him. Khan snatched away from him, but he turned the other way with Rock behind him.

I shook my head and grabbed the mic from Khanna, "I have a ton of games for us to play and at the end, after everybody eats, we will reveal the gender," I said then walked off.

I wasn't worried about the fact that nobody was coming with gifts, because Rich and I had gone out and grabbed everything the baby would need and then some.

*****

The night was progressing well and everybody was having a good time until Margo walked in looking like she was due any day. From that moment on, I knew everything was about to go from sugar to shit.

Rock got up and went to help her with find a seat. He then went to fix her a plate and took it to her. I scanned the room for Bam and sure enough her eyes were shooting daggers through the both of them while she was hugged up with Blake.

I guess Margo felt her gaze because once they made eye contact she stood up

"Oh goodness, Josiah! You didn't tell me she would be here! Take me home now!" she demanded.

I felt some shit brewing, but seeing Brooke walk in the door with KJ and Dae-Dae caught my attention. I looked to Khanna to gauge her reaction, she was smiling.

To say I was confused would be an understatement. KJ was clinging to Dae-Dae and smiling all the way. Brooke looked hella uncomfortable.

I saw Khan walking in their direction as if he was on the warpath, so I headed over too. "Why the fuck you touching on my son and shit?" Khan said grabbing KJ from Dae-Dae's grasp.

Dae'Sean didn't respond but instead looked at Brooke.

"Brooke why the hell you got this nigga holding my son and shit like I'm not even here and ya'll just one big happy family? You disrespectful, dick mouthed bitch!" Khan snapped handing KJ to Megan. Brooke didn't answer him either.

Khanna joined us and smirked at the both of them

"Hey baby daddy!" she said to Dae-Dae. This pussy ass nigga started shifting in his seat. "Nervous much," she spoke to both of them, "Well you should be. Now are you going to tell him Brooke or should I?"

Now I was even more confused than before.

"Tell me what?" Khan asked.

"That, that, umm, you're not KJ's father. Dae'Sean is," Brooke stammered.

Before she could say anything else, I pounced on that ass like a lioness on a gazelle. Everybody else can act like they missed it, but it was impossible not to notice the devastated expression on Khan's face.

This bitch had put me through hell and high water and KJ wasn't even Khan's son. I was so ready to kill this bitch. Just when I was getting over all the shit she had done to me in the past she drops another bomb. I felt Dae-Dae try to pull me off of her and then Khan dropped his ass.

"Don't touch my fucking wife nigga!" he snapped. It took Rich, Rock, and Kane to pull me off her ass.

We could never get together and do anything without some shit popping off. Khanna watched it all while laughing so hard she had to hold her stomach.

"You knew about this shit and you didn't say shit to me?" Khan asked her with hurt dripping from his voice. The look on Khanna's face said it all.

"Fuck you! The only sister I have from here on out is Bam."

He grabbed KJ from Megan and stormed out.

Chapter 21

Rich

"Watch yo muthafuckin' mouth when you talking to me nigga!" Alani called herself bucking on a nigga.

"Fuck all that shit you hollering about! How does it look if my bitch fighting over some shit that ain't got shit to do with her, but about some nigga she used to fuck with?" I asked her heated.

I look like a fucking dingbat on the sidelines while my bitch fought another bitch over her pussy ass baby daddy. I was heated when I found out the reason they were scrapping was because Khan.

"You don't understand! That bitch wreaked havoc in my life only for her son to not to be related to my daughter! She knew the whole time that KJ wasn't Khan's son, but she still acted like he was only to destroy my life! She even made him a Jr. Khan and I were fine for the most part until that shit happened!" she defended.

"So you still wanna be with that nigga?" I asked her.

To me it sounded like she was mad that they weren't still together. The hesitation she exhibited in answering my question was all I needed.

"Yo, I'm out. It's obvious you need some time figure some shit out," I told her, grabbed my keys and headed out the door.

Knowing La'La she wasn't going to chase behind me, not that I wanted her to. Instead I just grabbed a hotel room. Blake and I had a show coming up that I needed to have a clear head for in order to murder the set.

*****

The day of the showcase came and the whole city came out to show a nigga love. Blake and I had been doing this music shit for years, so a lot of the cats that had bought mixtapes from us before had been hipped to the hot fire we spit.

Blake and I stepped on stage and killed the set. We had only performed on a small level before, so to see this many people come out had us a little geeked up. Even though I ain't rocking with La'La like that right now, I'm forever grateful for her setting me and my nigga up with a chance like this.

Right before we stepped off the stage, bitches literally started throwing their panties at us. I didn't know people really did shit like that. I thought that shit only happened in movies. None of them hoes had shit on Alani, so I kept it moving.

Adonis and Envy had gotten us dressing rooms so I made my way to mine. I closed the door and made me a Henny on the rocks. I heard my door open and close; I turned around and made eye contact with an ebony colored beauty. Her inviting eyes were the color of emeralds. I downed my Hennessey, never breaking eye contact as she stripped down to her birthday suit.

"I've been watching you and your friend do ya'll thing since I was a youngin'. I've always been too shy to approach you, but not anymore," she said looking like a sexy demon.

I couldn't say anything, my words were caught in my throat as I stared at her flawless and blemish free body. She walked over to me and sat my glass down on the vanity, then pushed me down on the small love seat. She straddled me and removed my shirt. She kissed down the length of my chest until she got to my pants. Even if I wanted to stop her I couldn't, the drinks I had before the show combined with the ones I had after had my reaction time off. The Emerald Ebony unbuckled my pants and all in one motion she had my dick in her mouth.

She was deep throating without gagging, and that was a plus in my book. My head rolled back and I was in bliss. At that moment nothing else mattered. I felt myself about to bust so I pulled her up. She grabbed one of the magnums from the vanity and rolled it on with her mouth. She straddled me again and eased herself down my shaft. Her pussy welcomed me with open arms and held my dick in a bear hug. I had to pause for a moment to prevent premature ejaculation.

I must have paused too long cause she started riding me like her life depended on it; bucking and twirling her hips to a beat all her own. She shoved one of her breasts in my mouth and I sucked it. Her nipples looked like Hershey kisses and they tasted like them as well. The Emerald Ebony was working me too damn good so I knew I had to put in some work.

I flipped her over and slid in from behind.

"Oh shit daddy, right there that's my spot," she screamed out in ecstasy.

I looked down to see that her juices had coated the condom giving me motivation to go for broke in her pussy.

"I'm coming baby!" she screamed.

"Alright I'm right behind you," I exploded in the condom and collapsed on her back out of breath.

"Ayo Ma, what's your name?" I asked her.

Chapter 22

Bam

Shit had been going good between me and Blake, I haven't even been thinking about Rock. Blake finally got some pussy last night and I've been floating ever since. Plus, that nigga broke me off again before he left that morning. I had to soak in my Jacuzzi to soothe my vajayjay because I couldn't walk straight.

I had a hair appointment with La'La and Khanna but a knock at the door disrupted my process. I opened the door and was greeted by the last person I wanted to see.

"What the hell do you want?" I asked Mrs. Blondie, my psychiatrist.

I know what you're thinking, "Bam must be crazy," but I'm far from it. I battle a lot of demons on a daily basis and when I love, I love hard. Rock has always been able to bring out the worst in me. I think it's because I loved him so much. Shit who am I kidding? I still do. People think because I'm so hard that I don't have feelings under my tough girl exterior.

"You missed our last three sessions so I just decided to stop by," she responded with a smile on her face.

I moved to the side and let her in because knowing Mrs. Blondie, she wasn't budging.

She made herself comfortable in my sitting room and I followed suit.

"You can go ahead and lay back. I'm going to try to reach into your subconscious and unlock some of the things that you have trouble remembering from your early childhood."

I laid back on my chaise and closed my eyes. Shortly after listening to her voice I drifted off into another place.

"Mommy I don't want to do it anymore," I cried to my mother.

"You want to make mommy happy don't you?" she asked me.

"Yes," I cried even more.

"Okay baby, I promise this will be the last time. You know mommy loves you right?" she asked me.

"Yes" I replied again.

"Okay, so go in there and make momma proud.

She pushed me inside of the room and there were two men sitting inside already. Both of them looked nasty and made my young stomach churn. I guess they sensed the apprehension because the older one spoke up.

"It's okay lil' mama, come here," he signaled me with his ashy fingers.

I moved closer to him and he told me to open my mouth. I complied and he stuck his nasty finger in my mouth, rubbing something on my gums. A feeling of euphoria washed over me. My feet were planted in the spot that I was standing in and I couldn't move.

Next thing I knew was that the skimpy dress my mother had dressed me in was on the floor beside my feet and I was being led over to the raggedy mattress that was on the floor in the corner. I could see some of the springs sticking up and out of it. But the feeling that took over my body wouldn't allow me to protest nor put up a fight

The younger looking guy of the two put his hand between my legs and stuck my underdeveloped breast in his mouth. He spit on my vagina, stuck his penis at my opening and shoved it in. I would have screamed out in pain if it wasn't for the other guy sticking his little shriveled up ding-a-ling in my mouth. No matter how many times my mama subjected me to this torture my body was still not used to it. The things they were doing to my young body should have been a crime, in fact they were a crime.

In that moment, I hated my mother for allowing this to happen to me. This is the type of shit that she was supposed to protect me from, not expose me to. Yet here I was getting violated in every way possible, addicted to a drug that I didn't even know the name of.

Seconds later, I was staring up at the celling in my house.

"Good! Now I think that you have suppressed a lot of the feelings of hatred that you have for your mother and when you get mad you just lash out towards whomever it was that pushed your buttons."

"That's a possibility," was my only response.

The only reason I sought professional help was because I thought I had killed Rock. I felt a sense of relief when I had seen him alive, in the flesh. I remember bits and pieces of that night, but the rest is a blur.

"Well, you look like you're in a rush and I don't want to hold you up, but I think we've made lots of progress. In two weeks, we'll pick right up where we left off," Blondie said gathering her things after she jotted a few notes down on her notepad.

I walked her to the door and went to continue getting dressed for our girl's day out. I definitely need it.

Chapter 23

Rock

I could have killed Bam and that nigga when I saw him feasting on some shit I still believed to be mine. I just don't trust that nigga for some reason.

Khan and I were at our main trap just chopping it up. So much shit had been going on lately and we'd put our business on the back burner by letting some of our runners handle shit. For their sake, everything had run smoothly and we had no hiccups.

"Yo Khan, let me rap to you real quick."

We stepped to the side of the trap house.

"How you feel about that nigga Blake?" I asked him.

"What you mean?" he asked me feigning dumb.

"You know what I mean, nigga," I responded throwing a playful jab at him.

"I mean for real I don't give a fuck about that nigga either way," he said stroking his goatee.

"I'm saying though I don't trust that nigga and I really don't trust his ass around Sophie," I told him truthfully.

"Oh, so this is about Bam's lil crazy ass," he said like he had reached an ah ha moment.

"Naw, I mean, not exactly. I know Bam can hold her own, but I just don't like the nigga. His eyes hold too much deception," I stated.

"Nigga you know Bam will body a nigga for coming at her wrong, so you have nothing to worry about," Khan tried to reassure me.

I just hoped for Blake's sake that he was right.

*****

Finally, the day came for Margo to give birth to my son and I couldn't be happier. The only people in attendance besides Margo and myself were Aunt Megan, Uncle Kane, Khan, and Margo's mother. Everybody else was Team Bam, so nobody else came. At 6:32 PM, I got the shock of my life. Instead of the little boy we had been preparing for, I was blessed with a princess.

Josiana Rokiyah Thomas shocked all of us with her presence; weighing seven pounds seven ounces and twenty-two inches long. She's going to be tall just like her mama. This is a moment that I wished was being shared with Bam, but I was still happy about my baby girl.

"Congrats my nigga, she looks just like you," Khan said dapping me up.

Margo's mother hugged me and thanked me, which was weird because I had never met her before.

Aunt Megan came over and looked at the baby, but didn't touch her.

"You need to get a DNA test before you just start claiming the babies of random bitches," Megan spat.

"Chill out Auntie, I know this one here is mine," I assured her.

"Whatever boy, I'm not claiming her until I know for a fact she belongs to me," Megan turned up her nose and walked off. I just shook my head at her.

I knew I would need my aunt to watch my daughter one day so I told the doctor on the sneak that I would need a DNA test.

Right now nothing could take me off of the cloud that I was floating on.

Chapter 24

Khan

To watch my nigga have a baby brought out mixed emotions in me. I was happy for him, no doubt, but knowing that my son could possibly not be mine had me feeling crazy on the inside. I might not have been there when he was born, but ever since then I had been there.

When I grabbed him from my mother's arms and left Khanna's gender reveal party, I took him home with me. I was pissed off at my sister for not telling me and making me look like a fool in front of a room full of people.

When I got KJ home I just looked at him while he slept. When he was a newborn, he looked just like me, but now I don't really see a resemblance. He looks just like Brooke with the exception of his eyes. Now that I compare the two, he has the eyes of that bitch ass nigga, Dae-Dae.

Still I wasn't going to believe it until I got him tested on my own. Part of me didn't want to do it because that would have made it completely real and I wasn't ready for that. KJ is my namesake and it would kill me to have to part ways with him, but I knew it would have to be done.

So before I went home, I got one of those over-the-counter DNA tests. I swabbed his mouth and mine and dropped them both in separate envelopes. I would mail that shit off later, but for now I was going to spend as much time as possible bonding with my son.

*****

I had sent the DNA samples off already, so now I was just playing the waiting game for the results. I've had KJ since all that shit went down and La'La just dropped Karizma off so I was taking them to the bounce house. Rock was busy with his new addition so I was rolling solo.

When I got there, I got my kids situated and sat back and watched them crawl around. Some little girl pulled one of Karizma's ponytails and made her cry. I jumped up and grabbed my daughter and followed the little girl with my eyes as she walked to whom I assumed was her mother.

"Yo shorty, your lil' girl pulled my daughter's hair. You need to watch her lil' bad ass better," I snapped walking over.

"Who the fuck you think you talking to, my daughter isn't bad?" she snapped back with her hands on her hips.

"A feisty lil' bitch I see. Just make sure you keep a better eye on ya lil' brat. Next time I won't be so nice," I said and walked away.

I wasn't about to argue with a bitch that wasn't even in my tax bracket.

I had enough of my kids being all around these little snot nosed bastards with no home training, so I gathered them up to take them to get something to eat. I made a mental note that when my estate was finished being built, I would buy them their own bounce house for the back yard. I didn't really like my kids being around other people's kids anyway.

I went to a little pizza place not too far from there and saw the same lady with the bad ass little girl. Ignoring her, I grabbed food for my kids and I took a seat. I felt a presence over me as I ate, so I looked up and made eye contact with shorty. She was actually kind of pretty and she talked proper, but with a hood edge to her. She had hips and ass for days and her skin was the same complexion as mine. The only thing I found unattractive about her was the black, pink, and purple braids she wore.

"I'm sorry for the way I acted earlier. My daughter ended up telling me she did pull your daughter's hair. Somalia come here," she called out to her daughter.

"Say sorry to her for pulling her hair," she demanded of her daughter.

"I'm sorry," she spoke in a small voice while hiding behind her mother's leg.

"Now go eat," she sent her daughter away.

"I didn't catch your name," she spoke to me.

"That's because I didn't throw it," I responded.

"You really are an asshole," she said with her nose turned up. "Well my name is Somaya," she continued.

I didn't bother to respond, I was hungry as a hostage considering the fact that I hadn't eaten all day.

"Well, you should hit me up sometimes and maybe we could hang out, throw the kids a play date or something," she said. I still didn't respond.

Somaya then wrote her number on a napkin and slid it to me before walking away. I grabbed it and slid it in my pocket. Once we were done eating we headed out. Life was finally good for a nigga and I wasn't tryna to change that anytime soon.

Chapter 25

Rich

It's like a nigga had turned into an overnight celebrity. When Adonis told me that he would turn Blake and I into stars I almost didn't believe him, but he had definitely shown and proved. Within months of signing our recording contract we were on a nationwide tour.

The longer I stayed away from La'La the more I started slinging dick. We had since made up, but that shit didn't make a difference to me. She wanted to come on tour with me, but I ended up talking her into staying home so she could be with Karizma and be there when Khanna had the baby any day now.

The amount of bitches that were around was in abundance and eventually it got hard to resist. I still fucked with my Emerald Ebony from time to time and even brought her on tour with me. She didn't mind me bringing another bitch in the bedroom. Some shit I knew would never fly with La'La. I told her straight up that I had a bitch at home and she respected it.

Now don't get me wrong, La'La is the best thing since sliced bread, but I knew that she still wasn't over her baby daddy, even though she wants to be. I refuse to sit around waiting for her to decide what she wants. So until she decides, I'm going to continue to do me.

"Baby, are you coming to bed? Me and Sunshine are getting bored playing with each other," Ebony said, which turned out to be her real name. That was all I needed hear. I threw back my D'usse V.S.O.P and dived into bed. Ebony sat on my face while Sunshine sucked my dick. This was the life and I didn't see it changing anytime soon.

*****

Adonis was throwing a celebration for all of his artists and I had Alani on my arm looking amazing. We were posing on the red carpet while the paparazzi flicked away. Envy had the venue decorated elegantly, she could have paid somebody to do it, but she insists on doing most things herself. One thing I can say about my girl, she doesn't hang around slouch bitches. Everybody pulls their own weight in whatever endeavors they choose.

Alani saw Bam, Envy, and them and skated off to converse while I mingled a bit. I saw Adonis and walked towards them and cringed when I saw him talking to Khan and Rock. It's like everywhere I go, them niggas are there. I ain't scared of their asses, but I prefer not to be in their presence, even though I know that's damn near inevitable.

I should have known they would be here considering La'La was cool with Adonis' wife. I headed over to them anyway, ain't no nigga about to scare me. I'd been waiting for the moment when I could off Khan's ass anyway, it was only a matter of time.

Chapter 26

Khan

When I saw Rich's pussy ass walking up, I made a great escape. I looked back to see him smirking like he had run me off. Little did he know I had been waiting for him to leave La'La's side. When he walked up alone, I knew that was my chance. I found her in the corner sipping champagne and chatting.

"Yo La, let me holla at you real quick," she looked at me like I was crazy, but ended up getting up to follow me after excusing herself from the ladies.

I lead her to the bathrooms and made sure no one was watching before I pulled her inside the woman's restroom. After ensuring no one was inside I locked the door.

"What are you doing Khan," she asked with lust filled eyes. She wanted me just as bad as I wanted her.

I grabbed both sides of her face, careful not to mess up her hair, and covered her lips with mine. She rejected me a little bit at first, but then she kissed me with a matching passion. Her soft hands pulled off the jacket to my tux and unbuttoned my shirt while never removing her lips from mine.

When my pants hit the floor, she turned around for me to unzip her dress. I took a moment to admire her beauty. You couldn't even tell that she had a baby unless you looked at the spread of her child bearing hips. I had a thirst that only my La'La could quench.

She sat on the vanity and signaled for me to move closer with her slender fingers. I stepped out of my pants and moved towards her with lighting speed. I hadn't had any pussy in a while. She spread her thick thighs and she wasn't wearing any panties just like I knew she wouldn't. Her center glistened with moisture.

I was in need of some pussy, but not before I knelt down to taste her. Most men complain about not liking thick girls, but the thighs of a thick girl are the best earmuffs. I slurped on La'La's kitty like it was the last supper.

"Damn Khan, you better eat this pussy," she moaned while grinding on my face and I obliged.

I held both her legs up and licked her from her ass back to her clit until she started trembling.

Her juices were dripping on the floor as she came down from her orgasmic high. I stood up, stepped out of my boxers, and plunged directly up in her box. I had to pause for a second, and relish the moment. It had been so long since I'd sampled the forbidden fruit between her legs.

I must have taken too long because she started bucking towards me. Who was I to deprive my wife of what she craved? I wrapped my arms around her legs while gripping her thighs.

"Oh fuck Khan! I missed this shit!" she cried while scratching my arms up.

Right when I felt her about to cum I pulled out and slapped my dick on her clit, then put it back it. I repeated the process a few times until she grabbed my face

"KHAN PULL IT OUT AGAIN AND I'MA FUCK YOU UP!" she snapped.

My bitch is a straight savage! I said fuck it and went balls to the wall. I beat La'La's box out the frame and she pulled my shirt completely off and started touching my inked up and sculpted chest. La'La started licking my chest and that only made me want to go harder.

She pushed me off of her and hopped down off of the sink, then sank to her knees and deep throated a nigga. Don't get me wrong, Alani's pussy is great, but her head game is PHENOMENAL! I gripped her hair slightly just to keep my footing as she slobbed a nigga down, it felt like her tonsils were pulling me in while she used her jaws to apply slight pressure.

Alani hates giving head even though she's good at it, so she started to slow down. Instead of pulling out of her mouth, I reached down to massage her jaw. That only made her go harder. Right before I came in her mouth, I pulled her up, bent her over the sink, and pushed back in from behind.

The sight of her ass clapping as I hit her from the back was beautiful. Alani used her pussy muscles to pull me in and there was no turning back. I coated her walls with my DNA, marking my territory. She would always be mine and there was nothing anybody could do to change that.

We cleaned each other up and got dressed, making ourselves look as presentable as possible. The hickeys on my chest and the ones on her neck were very visible. She grabbed some concealer out of her purse and covered her neck as best she could, and straightened out her hair. I took notice to how she refused to make eye contact with me.

I walked up behind her and wrapped my arms around her waist.

"I love you Alani, I always have and I always will," I whispered against her ear.

"I love you too Khan," she replied.

We both just smiled, made sure the coast was clear and left the restroom.

I headed over to the bar to get a drink when Somaya came up to me.

"Baby I been looking for you for almost an hour," she said.

"I was outside smoking," I told her grabbing my drink.

"Oh you do look high," she giggled.

I felt high, but it damn sure wasn't no Kush that had me feeling this way.

I had been kicking it with Somaya since she gave me her number. I knew that damn near everybody in attendance at this little shindig was going to have a date so I gave her a call, some money to buy a dress, and brought her along. Somaya hooked her arm in mine and I felt holes burning into my back.

I turned to make eye contact with Alani and I could see the flames dancing in her eyes from across the room. I just shook my head and walked away.

Chapter 27

Alani

I knew I shouldn't be mad because I came to the party with someone else, but to see Khan hugged up with another bitch had me thirty-eight hot. She was clinging to him like a child to a mother, and grinning in his face like she was as happy as a pig in slop.

A bitch like her had probably never snagged a baller in her life. Even though she was dressed in an expensive Vera Wang ball gown she still looked cheap. The beauty supply store tracks in her head looked dull and lifeless. She ruined her beautiful gown by pairing it with drug store accessories.

I smiled a little knowing that she didn't have shit on me. Khan was probably attracted to the fat ass she had dragging behind her. I shrugged my shoulders, ordered a new drink, and continued conversing with my girls. Fuck Khan's stupid ass, but one thing I can't deny is that, that nigga had some good dick. I clenched my thighs together just thinking about it.

*****

Yes, a celebration was in order! A bitch was finally divorced and it felt damn good. I had been tied down to a man that only cared for himself damn near half of my life. Now the only thing we had to do was co-parent.

Mrs. Fitz arranged it so we didn't have to go to court or file for separation. Khan helped too by not putting up a fight and just signing the papers.

Tonight me and my girls, with the exception of Khanna because she was on bed rest, were going to Chic to have a couple drinks. It was time to let my hair down and unwind.

Rich had been on some whole other shit since he had got signed, so I haven't been fucking with him like that. But let me find out he's on some good bullshit, then its curtains for his ass.

I refused to be a fool for another man that doesn't mean me any good. Especially a man that knows firsthand what I'd been through with Khan and his infidelities. I will personally hand Rich his balls if I find out he has some ill intentions with me.

*****

I was twerking in my seat while turning up with my team. I like to get loose a little bit, but I prefer Chic over a club any day considering it attracts a more mature crowd.

Envy leaned in my direction, "I saw you sneak off with Khan the other night, you're playing with fire."

"Girl, don't get me wrong, Rich can put it down; but Khan is on a whole 'nother level. The nigga dick is molded from gold and he hits spots that I didn't know existed, not that it's any of your business," I responded and then sipped my drink.

Now I fuck with Envy, but I don't need anybody attempting to lecture me on the decisions I make. My pussy misses Khan more than I care to admit to, hence the reason I put up no resistance.

"I'm just saying, you know I love you like the sister I wish I had, and I only want the best for you," Envy added.

"I know, but rest assured, I'm good and I got this covered," I said.

I guess she knew to leave well enough alone because she didn't bring it back up and I was grateful for that.

The rest of our night went off without a hitch and it felt good.

Chapter 28

Bam

Damn, I hadn't felt alive in I don't know how long. Blake had a bitch floating on a natural high daily. Every morning I got up with extra pep in my step, and he helped ease the pain of knowing Rock had another baby.

Blake didn't try to force me to do anything, everything between us just flowed so naturally. That fact that his sex was good was a plus in my book. Right now we were preparing to go to on a date only he wouldn't tell me where.

Once in the car, we greeted with a kiss, but we didn't say anything to each other for the duration of the ride. I sat vibing to the music unable to contain my excitement, anxious about finding out where we were headed.

Pulling up to Dave and Buster's, I burst into a fit of screams.

"AHH! Bae come on, let's go!" I screamed after kissing Blake.

The kid in me felt like I was in a candy store. I ran inside clinging to Blake waiting for him to load our cards. Once he handed me mine, I took off. I played every game I could before hunger pangs set in then, I went in search of Blake.

I saw him playing air hockey with some low budget bitch so I went over and made my presence known.

"I'm hungry let's go" I said and grabbed his arm pulling him with me.

He must not know I'm a territorial lioness, I don't play that shit. I did a lot of crazy shit when I was with Rock, so I've been trying to tone it down a bit; but just because I'm on a new block that doesn't mean that old bitch isn't right around the corner.

Blake didn't protest so I had no reason to show my ass. Once we were seated and our orders were placed, I turned to him.

"I'm sorry that I've kind of ruined our date. We are supposed to be spending time together, but instead I've been running around doing my own thing. I'm not making an excuse for it, but I had to grow up a lot faster than I should have," I stated putting my head down.

The shit I had to endure at the hands of my egg donor has basically ruled my life. All my life felt that I need to defend myself even if there is no physical threat. Despite what my mother put me through at such a young age, I always loved her and still do.

"You good baby girl, that shit ain't no slices out of my pie. I'm just happy you got to unwind, let your hair down, and have fun," he replied kissing my face.

I smiled relived that he didn't feel some type of way. Our food came and we made small talk until we were interrupted.

"You owe me a rematch," the old, off-brand chick from earlier came over and said to Blake.

"Umm, excuse me hoe, don't you see us eating," I asked her with much attitude.

"I was talking to your brother," she said then redirected her attention to Blake.

"Brother?" I responded perplexed.

"Stay out of grown folk's business lil' girl. How old are you? Like twelve?" she asked right before I pounced on her ass.

"Bitch how old do you think I am now? Huh hoe? How old do you think I am now!?" I screamed pistol whipping her with the strap I pulled from the small of my back.

Before I could do enough damage to make me feel better, I was being lifted into the air, but not by Blake.

"Chill out lil' sis," Khan said carrying me away.

He took me all the way outside and put me in the front seat of his truck. "Sit right here Bam, I'll be right back," he told me. I was tempted to go back in and finish that hoe off, but decided to listen to Khan and sit there. A few minutes later he came out with Somaya, the girl he had been kicking it with. They hopped in the back seat and he pulled off.

I was thirty-eight hot, so I grabbed the pre-rolled blunt from Khan's ashtray and flamed it up in attempt to calm my nerves. People always feel the need to test me. That bitch was trying to say that I looked young enough to be his sister. But don't let the height and baby face fool you. I bet that bitch will cross the street next time she sees me. I don't mind murking a nigga or bitch a like, but I love to do some hellified damage to their asses, so they can spread the word not to fuck with me.

"Here's your phone sis," Khan said handing me my iPhone 6.

I examined the screen and it was completely shattered. I know iPhone was tired of me ordering new phones. I couldn't stop breaking my phone to save my life.

I made eye contact with Somaya sitting in the back seat and turned up my nose. She was pretty in a pit bull kind of way, if you know what I mean. I guess Khan peeped game because he spoke up.

"Sis, this is Somaya. Mya, this is my sis Bam" he said trying to relieve some of the tension that was building up.

I've always hated how he brings so many of these temporary hoes around like they're going to be around long. He has always had a new flavor of the week or month since he and Alani split, but hey; it's none of my business.

"Nice to meet you, Bam" Somaya said, but I ignored her.

She wasn't my friend and I wasn't going to act like she was. That hoe couldn't sit with us.

I turned up the music to rap with Khan, without the wandering ears. It was time we started putting our personal shit to the side and made running our business a priority.

Chapter 29

Khan

I had been in a funk ever since I got a notice in the mail that my divorce had been finalized. The last thing I was about to do was sit around sulking over her, fuck that bitch. I had been kicking it with Somaya hard, so I was just going to pour all of my time and energy into seeing where shit was going with her.

I've been bonding with her daughter and she's a really sweet kid. Somalia has even helped out with my kids, her lil' ass thinks she's grown.

Today is her birthday, so I'm throwing her a lil' cookout at my mom's crib and letting her invite her lil' friends from school and around her neighborhood. It took a little convincing at first, but I talked my mom into cooking the food. My father said he would man the grill, so we were good.

I had let Kane's past slide... for now. Ain't no sense in making the nigga pay for some shit that was out of his hands. Once I actually sat down and listened to what the nigga had to say, I understood why he did what he did. When you live a certain lifestyle you have to be ready to deal with the consequences that come with it. Now even though it wasn't ideal for him to abandon his family, when shit happens you have make the best of it. He chose to protect his family and I can't do shit but respect that.

I had Somaya riding shot gun in the 2015 blacked out range rover I just copped. What's the point of grinding day in and day out it I can't enjoy the fruits of my labor? I had been putting our businesses on the back burner because of the personal shit, but I was back to grind mode.

Right now we're going to pick up some gifts for Somalia's party. I don't fuck with Alani, if it doesn't have anything to do with Karizma, but she had Khanna's gender reveal party decked out so I asked her to decorate my mama's back yard for me. She agreed, but I didn't tell her what it was for. It might be a fuck nigga move, but fuck it. Her feelings no longer mattered to me, they were for that nigga Rich to worry about.

***

Everything was in place and it looked great. My mom and my pops had shit smelling good. Now all we had to do was wait for everybody to arrive. Rock was coming with Margo, even though their baby was too new to play with any of the other kids. La'La was bringing my daughter and Brooke was bringing my son. Until I get the DNA tests back, he's my son and I would continue to treat him as such.

Everything was going great and the party was in full swing. I had to pat myself on the back for getting everything together. Shit like this ain't even a nigga's cup of tea. I just hoped for the sake of the kids that this crazy family of mine held their shit together.

I looked over and caught a glimpse of Rock shooting daggers in the direction Bam and Blake. Bam was sitting in his lap feeding him from her plate. I could see why my nigga was so mad. Bam had softened up since fucking with him. And I honestly didn't know whether it was a good or bad thing. But that shit wasn't none of my business any way. Somaya was running around after the kids making sure they were good. I made my way to her and grabbed a handful of her ass.

"Babe they're good come eat," I whispered against her ear then kissed her neck.

"Okay baby, I just wanted to make sure they were all good," she replied kissing my lips.

We walked away hand in hand toward the food table. I don't know what it was, but Somaya always felt the need hold my hand. I wasn't complaining though, she was holding a nigga down… for the time being.

I started making my plate then I heard a voice behind me "So, this is what you had me decorate for?"

I turned around to face La'La and it took everything in me not to laugh at the cute little scowl on her face, while she bounced Karizma on her hip.

"Yeah I needed help with setting up for lil' mama birthday," I told her and continued to make my plate.

"That's low Khan, even for you," she responded shaking her head.

"Whatever Ma, it is what it is. Thank you though," I told her.

Instead of responding she just slapped my plate out of my hand causing some of the food to fall on my shirt. Then she stormed off and sat down beside Khanna. I haven't been fucking with my sister either. She thought it was funny to hide the fact that KJ might not be my son and made me look like a fucking fool. She could have put me up on game ahead of time, but instead she chose to be messy about the situation.

I continued to make my plate, a nigga was hungry as a hostage and I didn't have time eat earlier. I sat down to eat and Somaya sat beside me. I was crushing until I felt a body standing over me. I looked up and locked eyes with my mother. I sighed knowing she was about to be all up in my business.

"Can I have a word with my son in private?" My mama asked with much attitude.

"Sure Ms. Megan," Somaya said and walked off.

She found a table that nobody was sitting at and finished eating her food. Megan cleared her throat, so I turned my attention back to her.

"You need to get yo' shit together Khan," she said.

"I usually try to stay out of your business, but I'm a woman first. I didn't raise you to be out here making babies with all these women. Now don't get me wrong there is no problem with you wanting to throw a party for her little girl, but to get your wife..." she said before I cut her off.

"Ex-wife."

"…well, ex-wife to decorate a party for the daughter of your new bitch is low and you need to tighten that shit up before I fuck you up my damn self," she mushed me and walked away.

I just shook my head, I didn't know what I was going to do with the women in my life.

The party was winding down and everybody pitched in to clean up. I heard Alani, Bam, and Khanna start laughing.

"Babe I'm ready to go," Somaya came up to me and said.

"We can't just leave all this shit for my mama to clean herself. Plus, she said she'd watch all the kids tonight, even Somalia," I told her grabbing a bag of trash.

"Well, I'll be in the car waiting for you then. I'm not going to sit here and listen to these bitches keep talking shit about me," Maya pouted with her arms folded.

I sighed and rubbed my hands through my dreads. The last thing I wanted to do was get in between some petty little rivalry with my new girl and my old girl.

"Ignore them, you're here with me right?" I asked her.

"Yeah, I'm here with you," she smiled.

"Iight then, now let's finish cleaning up so I can beat that pussy out the frame when we get to the crib."

"Alright daddy," she smirked walking away and I smacked her ass.

Just as Somaya walked away, Bam walked up.

"Damn, bro you sure know how to pick em'," she said.

Before I could respond Maya hit an about-face and made her way back to where we were, I guess she heard what Bam had said.

"And what's that supposed to mean?" Somaya asked Bam.

I just knew this wasn't about to be pretty. Bam not being one to ever back down replied with a smirk "It means you're ugly."

"Baby, I'm far from ugly" Maya argued.

By this time Alani and Khanna had made their way over as well.

"Bitch please, you are closer than you think," Bam countered making Alani and Khanna snicker with glee.

I assumed that was what they were laughing about earlier.

"What the fuck y'all laughing at?" Maya snapped in their direction.

"Baby, this ain't what you want," Khanna said.

"Your ugly ass," Alani told Maya.

"Y'all bitches wish I was ugly. Y'all just mad that he's with me," Maya said still trying to defend herself.

Now I didn't think Maya was ugly, she just wasn't the pick of the litter. They were just being petty because without a doubt she can't hold a candle to La'La. There was no denying that, La'La was a bad bitch. She used to be my bad bitch until she divorced a nigga. Then it was fuck that bitch!

"Ain't nobody mad he's with your ugly ass. You can put makeup on a pig and it's still going to be a pig. Plus, he's had an abundance of ugly bitches before you, and you don't wanna know what's happened to some of them," Alani said and walked away.

The Dynamic trio walked into the house to say their goodbyes to moms, pops, and the kids then walked out the front door leaving me and Maya to finish cleaning up everything. If only Maya had shut the fuck up and ignored them like I said, we would be good. I'm not even talking about the cleaning. This bitch had just made it awkward for every family function that we have. She doesn't know my baby mama and her crew like I do and them broads are a force to be reckoned with.

***

"I called this meeting to let you all know that I'm proud of y'all. I had to step back and take a brief hiatus, but I'm back now and I don't plan on leaving again anytime soon."

"Mont and Ron, I'm promoting y'all niggas. Y'all held shit down while we handled other business. I checked the books and y'all were never once short. For now on anything y'all need will be obtained through them. They will be in direct contact with me and/or Rock, we'll send orders through them. But on another note I got bonuses for everybody around the table. Y'all niggas worked hard and you deserve it," I told everybody.

Even though I ain't rocking with Alani, it felt good to have her back in her rightful place at the round table. Business still went smoothly when she and Bam were going through their shit and having babies, but I know it could have been smoother if they were around. Those bitches were straight thorough and most, if not all, the niggas out here feared them.

I dismissed the meeting and Alani jumped up from the table and headed back to the office. I got up and followed her. We were about to be making more money than we knew what to do with and I needed her back on board whether we were in a relationship or not.

"What's your problem," I asked her as soon as the door to the office shut.

"Nothing, Khan. Leave me alone and go check on your bitch. I'm sure her feelings are still hurt," she said with her lip poked out.

La'La always did that shit when she was felling some type of way.

"Ohh, so that's what this is all about," I said like I had a revelation of some kind.

"No, I'm fine Khan, so you can just go," she said and folded her arms across her chest like a defiant child.

I moved swiftly across the room and invaded her space. I wrapped my arms around her hands traveling to her ass.

"Move Khan," she said, but didn't put up much resistance. I took that as my queue to pick her up and she wrapped her legs around my waist as I knew she would. La'La seems to think she is fat, but I know better. She only weighs 210 pounds and that was after giving birth to my shorty.

I kissed her lips and when I went to pull back she took my lip into her mouth sucking on it. She could act like she was so happy with that nigga Rich if she wanted to, but I knew better. That nigga wasn't treating her pussy right. Still holding onto her, she started kissing and sucking on my neck; La'La knew that was a nigga spot low-key.

I swiped everything off the desk and sat her on top. She had a dress on, which I knew she didn't have panties on underneath. I lifted her dress until it was around her waist. She was staring at me with lust filled eyes, right before I dove in. La'La loves head more than any bitch I've ever been with. I sucked on her clit applying just the right amount of pressure to her g-spot with my middle finger.

I know Alani's body like the back of my hand, possibly even better than she does. Just as she was about to cum, I stopped and slid into her honey pot. Her pussy started squirting on my dick as I moved in and out of her, soaking my shirt and stomach along the way. I pulled my shirt from over my head and tossed it, then stepped out of my pants, while still beating her shit up. I kissed her deeply so she could taste how sweet she tasted. I don't be eating random hoes' pussies, but La'La's shit tasted like a sweet forbidden fruit that hasn't been discovered.

"Damn Daddy, right there. Ohh fuck," she moaned.

"Shut the fuck up," I snapped.

"You want me to leave you alone right?" I asked her.

Hitting her spot just the way she liked it.

"No, I don't," she moaned out trying to fuck me back.

"Stop moving! But you divorced me though right?" I asked her making her squirt again.

"I'm sorry, I didn't mean too," she moaned out.

I knew she was only saying that shit because of the dick lashing I was putting on that ass.

"You still love a nigga?" I asked her.

"Yessss!" she screamed out as an orgasm ripped through body.

I looked down and her pussy had a nigga's dick coated with her essence. I had to draw my eyes away to keep from bussing.

"I want to hear you say it," I told her nearing my peak as well.

"I Loveee you Khann!" She screamed as her body succumbed to the pleasure I unleashed.

I bust all up inside of her, because as far as I was concerned this pussy was and will always be mine. Alani's shit still fits me like a glove.

"I love you too," I kissed her forehead and then her lips.

I helped her up and we both hopped into the shower that was in our joint office. We started to clean up but not before going for round two.

Chapter 30

Alani

I woke up one morning to Rich creeping his dirty ass into the house. That nigga had been acting real funny since he got that record deal. I got out of bed without saying shit to him.

"Good morning, love," he said trying to kiss me, but I moved out the way so he only caught my cheek.

"Damn, I been on tour for three months and I can't get no love?" he asked me.

"Brush your fucking teeth first," I snapped.

Instead of waiting for him to respond, I walked into the bathroom and turned on the shower. I applied my facial mask, brushed my teeth, and stepped into the shower.

Rich came into the shower and hugged me from behind.

"I missed you baby," he whispered against my ear.

"I missed you too," I smirked because he couldn't see my face.

He started rubbing my body starting a fire I didn't want him to put out, but my body did.

I didn't want to look in his face, so I bent over and made sure my arch was just right. He slid in with precision and it made me wince just a little bit. My pussy was still sore from fucking with Khan and his big dick, but I sucked it up.

I threw my ass back into Rich to hurry and get this shit over with. When he finally released I was relived. I washed my body and got out. Now don't get me wrong, when I first started fucking with

Rich he did my body justice; but the couple of times that I crept with Khan made me realize why I stayed so long.

That nigga's dick was just magical. I swear he had the Krabby Patty secret formula embedded in his shit. I shuddered and had to clench my thighs to ward off the thoughts of Khan. To get him off my mind I had to remind myself that he's fucking with that dog faced, duck mouthed bitch, Somaya.

I laughed to myself thinking of how she looked when we fired her ass up at her daughter's birthday party. There isn't a jealous bone in my body, but that girl is butt ass ugly. Thinking she looks good with them black, pink, and purple braids in her hair. She talked so proper, but her attitude and persona screamed hood rat.

I didn't trust that bitch, but she hasn't done anything yet to make me want to beat her ass, so I decided to let her live for the time being.

*****

Khanna called me saying she felt like she was in labor, so I got Rich to watch Kay-Baby for me so I could take her to the hospital. I called Bam, Envy, and Megan so that they could meet me up at the hospital.

When we got there, she was already in active labor and completely dilated. It didn't take long before she pushed her son into this cruel world.

Khan was still being a bitch and was mad at his sister, but he put his bullshit aside to be there for his nephew's birth.

Kadir Macario Thomas was born weighing nine pounds and ten ounces. He was big as hell no wonder Khanna was on bed rest the majority of her pregnancy. His name meant *powerful* and *to be blessed* and that he will be. The Thomas' don't fold in the face of adversity. We stick it out and make the best of each situation that comes to pass.

We were all sitting around ogling the new addition to the Thomas clan when Dae'Sean burst in the room. We always have to go through some bullshit when we all get together, and I knew this time would be no different than the rest.

"So you couldn't call and tell me that you were having the baby?" Dae'Sean asked Khanna. I rolled my eyes at him, I couldn't stand that nigga. To me he's a fuck boy and Brooke was a professional home wrecker. That chick just couldn't get enough of sleeping with a man that was already spoken for.

"No, actually I couldn't. Don't you have a baby already that you can go and check on?" She asked him.

I looked over at Khan and saw his jaw twitch, I was about to make my way over to him to calm him down right before shit went down.

"Bitch…" was all Dae-Dae got out before Kane pounced on his ass. It was like a lion attacking a gazelle.

"Pussy nigga! Disrespect my daughter again and I will end you!" Kane snapped beating Dae-Dae's ass.

I knew this hospital was tired of us. We were always fighting in it. Khan broke it up before it could go any further. Together they dragged him into the hallway and we continued to celebrate our new addition.

***

"I'm going to kill this fuck nigga!" I said to myself.

I went to use the bathroom after waking up and my fucking pussy was on fire. Not to mention the foul odor that was coming from it. I just knew Khan's dirty dick ass had given me something.

I called my OBGYN and she managed to squeeze me in immediately. I got dressed and headed straight there with steam coming out of my ears I was so mad. I signed myself in and was escorted straight to the back. When I got into the exam room I stripped down, put on the paper gown, and got onto the exam table. I wasn't wasting anytime.

When my doctor came in and saw that I was ready, she said, "Good morning, Mrs. Thomas, since you're ready, let's get right to it. You've already had your annual visit since you had the baby, so what brings you in today?" she asked me.

"I woke up and used the restroom and my vagina was burning something terrible and it smelled disgusting," I told her as she gave me a pap smear.

"Okay, so according to the symptoms you've mentioned, it sounds like you may have chlamydia. I won't know until I get your results back, but I'm going to prescribe you the medication to treat it. If you don't have it, it won't have any harmful effects on you," my doctor said finishing up my exam. I thanked her, grabbed the prescription, got dressed, and left. My first stop was the pharmacy, my second was a visit to Khan.

Chapter 31

Khan

Bang! Bang! Bang! Somebody was banging on my front door like the police. I snatched the door open and came face to face with a pissed off Alani.

"You busy?" she asked with a scowl on her face.

"Naw, come in," I held the door open for her.

"You can go in the living room, I'll be right in there," I told her.

I headed to the kitchen to grab a bottle of water, because she interrupted my workout knocking on my door.

I turned around, but was met with Alani's closed fist. Out of reflex, I smacked the shit out her. That shit didn't matter though because she followed up with a left that stunned my ass. She must have been really pissed about something because she hailed blow after blow to my face and chest. She was swinging so wildly I couldn't restrain her, before long we were getting our Ike and Tina on in the middle of my living room.

When I finally grabbed both of her arms and pinned them down to her sides, we both laid on the floor spent like we had been through a round of rough sex. My left eye felt like it was swollen shut. Alani's hair was wildly spread about her head, her lip was bust and she had a huge bruise forming on her cheek from where I slapped her.

"What the fuck is your problem girl?" I finally got the chance to ask.

"You burned me, you friendly dirty dick bitch!" she screamed trying to get away from me, but placed my weight down on her rendering her immobile.

"My dick clean girl, you wanna taste it?" I teased attempting to lighten the mood.

I know that everybody's symptoms can be different, but neither Maya nor myself have had any problems and as of lately we had been going raw squirrel.

"Well nigga, my burning pussy says otherwise" she countered "so I suggest you and your bitch go get checked."

I could tell that she had calmed down so I let her up. "Whatever girl, hit me up when you get them results," I told her then showed her to the door.

It was then I noticed she had on brass knuckles. I knew I didn't have shit, but just for good measure I was going to go get checked and Maya was going with me.

*****

A doctor's visit led to us finding out that Maya was pregnant, but STD free. Fuck my life! I don't want no more kids right now, but I'm going to be there for my seed regardless.

I plan on doing shit right this time around so I had her move out of her lil apartment and in with me. I had also made shit official with her and her daughter had started calling me daddy.

I had a problem with that shit at first, but eventually I let it go. There was no sense in feeling some type of way when I did everything a father would do for her wanna be grown ass. I told

Maya to leave all her lil raggedy shit at her old place and I bought her a whole new wardrobe.

I couldn't have a bitch on my arm that didn't match my fly. I tried to let her go shopping on her own, handing her some money but she had bought a whole bunch of bullshit. That bitch had gone to Rainbow's and spent two stacks on some cheap ass clothes. I made her take all that shit to a local woman's shelter to give them something to be happy about.

I made her give her raggedy van to her ratchet cousin and her three bad ass kids, so they wouldn't have to keep calling asking for rides, and bought her an infinity truck.

Since finding out about her being pregnant, she had quit her little nursing job to stay at home all day. Which I didn't mind… for now because I make enough money for a whole school of people. I just hoped I didn't live to regret my decision.

Chapter 32

Megan

I had forgiven Kane for his past indiscretions and we were in a happy space. Words couldn't describe the feeling I felt once he and Khan made up and got to know each other. Kane can't get back the time he lost with his son, but he sure was starting to build something with him.

I'm glad they were good because I was tired of trying to keep this family afloat on my own. It was time for Kane to pick some of that weight up. Kane tends to all of his grandkids so attentively. I think it's partially to make up what he lost with his kids.

KJ and Karizma were walking and getting into everything with Karizma as the ring leader. I couldn't fathom how lost I would be if KJ turned out not to be my son's. I would still want to be in his life. Brooke had to be the worst type of bitch there was. First, you get pregnant by a nigga that got a girl, only to reveal that it ain't his baby, but another nigga's baby that also has a girl, who is supposed to be your friend.

I could never understand how a chick could fuck with a nigga knowing he has a girl. I can't even remember how many girl's asses I had to stomp a mud hole in for fucking with Kane back in the day. It wasn't until I got older that I realized how stupid I looked.

Fighting over a piece of dick is never a good look, and that's what I try to instill into Khanna, Bam, and Alani. I never looked down on them when they would tell me when they did fight over the men in their lives, because I once did the same thing.

But I've been there, done that, and got the t-shirt. Fighting over a man that can't keep his dick in his pants makes you look like a fool in the end; it's better to just leave. Men, or should I say boys, need to learn their lessons, because it usually goes like this. You with a nigga, he cheats, you beat his side chick's ass, he apologizes, you take him back, and the cycle repeats.

You can't keep a nigga that doesn't want to be kept, at some point you have to put your foot down and let a nigga know that you're not the one to be fucked over. Then you also can't go around fighting whatever bitch he sleeps with behind your back. That hoe doesn't owe you any loyalty, your man does. It took me years to understand that.

Now what I can understand is a female fighting a chick that KNOWS a man has a woman and she still chooses to sleep with him. That is the bitch that needs her baby maker carved out. That's the worse type of hoe there is.

I had to learn to love me enough not allow Kane to break my heart time after time. Before he skipped town on me, I had left his ass. I packed my kids up and got me a hotel room. I didn't tell Kane where we were nor did I contact him. Not that I was trying to keep Khan and Khanna away from him, but I couldn't see his face for fear that I would succumb to his charm and melt the ice I was forming around my heart when it came to him.

He had to work hard to show me that he deserved to be with a woman like me. I had to become strong and even though I took him back again, he didn't step out on me anymore, well at least to my knowledge.

Since Kane was back in my life I hoped for his sake he didn't fuck up. I wasn't the same woman he once knew. I had no more fucks left to give when it comes down to it. See I'm the type of person that can deal with a new mistake every day, because regardless of how old we are, each day is still a learning experience. But what I refuse to deal with is someone who continuously makes the same mistake, which was unforgivable in my eyes.

Now that my family is in a good space I can rest easy knowing that there isn't anybody out here trying to cause us harm.

Chapter 33

Khanna

Since I had my precious baby Kadir, I hadn't wanted to do anything besides stay cooped up my house and love on him. We never got to reveal the gender at my gender reveal party. La'La just went ahead and told me what I was having. I'd been breast feeding because they said in the long run it helps with weight loss and I was at the very least trying to snap back to my pre-pregnancy size.

I hadn't heard from Dae-Dae since he got his ass handed to him by my father at the hospital the day Kadir was born, not that I was mad about it. I know I'll have to see and talk to him sooner or later, but for right now I'm content without seeing him. I'm still not over him being the father of Brooke's son, in addition to them sleeping around again.

On top of that, my brother hasn't been fucking with me like that since my party. He wasn't going to believe that KJ wasn't his son until he got the results back from a test that he'd done on his own. I couldn't blame him for that though, he'd been raising that little boy as his own since a little bit after he was born.

I love that little boy too, but after what I know now, I can't look in his face without feeling some type of way. He has same exact eyes as Dae'Sean and I can't stomach that shit. I knew I would get over it eventually and when that did happen I still wanted to be in his life.

I mean me and Brooke used to be virtually inseparable, I used to call her my sister, so I would still consider him my nephew even if he turned out not to be Khan's son.

*****

"Turn up bitch!" Bam screamed pushing her way inside my house, followed by Alani and Envy.

"I hoped you pumped, because we getting fucked up tonight!" La'La added.

"If you didn't I got the strips for you to test your milk before giving it to him," Envy said handing me the milk test strips, not that I needed them.

I had already pumped and froze or refrigerated enough milk to last him for at least a day or two. Kadir was down for a nap, so for the time being we didn't have to worry about him.

I grabbed all of the little finger foods I'd prepared for the occasion and sat them on the table in the den. I grabbed all the liquor and took it in the kitchen. I pulled out my Nutribullet and made us all mixed drinks. We made a vow that regardless of what we were going through that we would get together at least once of month for a little girl's night.

I brought everybody's drink out and took a seat. I noticed the bruise on La'La's face even though she tried to cover it with a pile of make-up.

"What the fuck happened to your face?" I shrieked.

"I don't want to talk about it. Next subject," she responded avoiding eye contact.

I was going to leave it alone, but I should have known that it wasn't going to fly with Bam.

"Oh hell naw! Who the fuck did that to your face?" Bam snapped holding the side of La'La's face.

We all were staring in her direction waiting for her to dish the tea. "I was fighting with Khan."

"Come on y'all we gotta go fuck his ass up now!" Bam said pulling out her gun.

"Wait y'all begged me to tell you, now you got to wait for me to finish, that's not all," she said shocking us all.

"I've slept with Khan twice since we've broken up; once at the party Adonis and Envy threw and again at the warehouse when we had a meeting," She said.

"Bitch we already knew that," I laughed and Bam and Envy high-fived me then each other.

Alani cut her eyes at us, sparked a blunt, and then took a sip of her drink before continuing.

"Well, I woke up one day with my pussy on fire, so I went to the doctor. I knew I had something. Khan was the first person to come to mind because of his history. Come to find out, I had chlamydia, so went to go beat his ass. Long story short, Khan showed me his and Somaya's clean bills of health."

"Well, where did you get it from if not from Khan?" I asked and we all wore curious expressions on out faces.

"Rich," was her one-worded reply.

We all looked on with shocked expressions on our faces. Rich was such a good guy you would never think that he would be the culprit.

"He was the last person that I had slept with and you know something crazy thing? We fucked and that nigga ain't said shit about having a hot dick since then," she said shaking her head.

"I haven't said anything to him yet, but he will feel my wrath soon. He's let this newfound fame go to his head, but I'm going to singlehandedly bring him back down to size.

I sat speechless not knowing what to say. Envy changed the subject and we all just chilled for the rest of the night. I swear all of our lives are drama-filled, but on everything I love I wouldn't trade these hoes for nothing in this world.

Chapter 34

Rich

Damn, I knew I had messed up. When I took a piss and my dick was burning I knew that I had fucked up royally. I strap up with all these hoes I fuck on the road with the exception of my Emerald Ebony, but the one time I don't, it comes back to bite me in my ass. I was fucking with some lil' bitch and I was about to put on a condom, but she climbed on top and that pussy felt so good that couldn't make her hot pussy ass get up.

That little sexcapade led to me and Ebony at the clinic getting treated. I wish I would have found out before I went home and fucked with my old lady. A nigga doesn't even know how to approach her about the situation, but she hasn't said shit to me and I damn sure ain't said shit to her.

I made Ebony catch an UBER while I drove home in deep thought. I didn't even have the radio playing, it was just me and my thoughts. I pulled into the driveway happy that all the lights were off. I got in the house and after looking around I noticed she wasn't even home.

That bought me a little bit of time to come up with a lie she would believe, because La'La is far from dumb. I took a shower and hopped in the bed to catch some z's. I didn't even bother putting any clothes on. Before long I was out for the count.

*****

I woke up and tried to roll over only to see that I was tied to the bed. I turned to the side and there it was, blown up poster size for me to see: her test results of a STD screening, positive for chlamydia.

I had seen Alani in action and the shit she does can bring even a grown man to his knees. The last place I've ever wanted to be in life is on the receiving end of her fury. A series of events that I had always been in complete control over had landed me there.

I started to try to free myself, but Alani had a military style knot in this damn rope. She walked into the room shortly after, wearing an outfit that made her look like a dominatrix. That shit was low-key sexy as hell. She had on a Swarovski crystal encrusted caged monokini, holding a leather whip and a serving tray.

Whap! She slapped me across the face with the leather whip.

"I think you know why you're here, so there is no need for me to debrief you on that," she spoke evenly.

"Baby, let me explain," I said attempting to formulate a lie. Whap!

"No need, feeling like I had a Hot Pocket in my pussy was all the explanation I needed. Since you felt the need to give me something, it's only right that I return the favor."

The sinister smile that graced her face had a nigga ready to shit himself. When she removed the lid on the serving tray I died twice before I came back to life. She had an array of knives and other unsavory items.

"Try not to scream," she laughed like the joker.

She pulled out a chrome butterfly knife and sliced me across my chest so quick I never saw it coming.

"Damn, the man at the store said this was a good one, but I didn't think it was that sharp," she exclaimed.

She cut me so many times across my chest that I became numb to the pain. That was until she pulled out a blow torch.

"You burned me, so now I'm gonna burn you," she took the blow torch to my chest and I screamed bloody murder. The burning sensation along with my open wounds felt like I had fallen into the deepest pits of hell.

She started to move towards my dick with the blow torch which made my eyes grow as big as saucers.

"La'La noooo!" I screamed which caused her to smile.

"Now I'm going to let you sit here and marinate in your own thoughts. Maybe next time you will at the very least strap up, to keep from bringing anything home to me," with that she walked out of the room leaving me tied up.

I was in so much pain, but from what I could see they were all flesh wounds. Eventually I succumbed to it and passed out. When I woke up I was still in bed, but I was no longer naked. I had on sweats, my chest had been patched up, and I was no longer tied up. I knew one thing my girl had set me straight for life.

■■■

■■■

Chapter 35

Alani

I knew I probably shouldn't have been so mad at Rich considering I was fucking Khan, but I didn't bring anything home to him. That nigga was out in the streets really feeling himself. Those groupie hoes he got running behind him must have gotten to his head.

After calling the hood doctor to come stitch his simple ass up and treat his burns, I left to go get my hair done. Fucking with Rich had made me late for my appointment with Diamond.

***

I'm far from an ugly bitch, so I was more than used to heads turning when I stepped into the room. I walked into Heavenly Touch with my Christian Dior's clicking across the floor. My Juicy Couture perfume greeted the receptionist before I did. "Hello, how are you? I'm here to see Diamond, I have a twelve o'clock appointment," I spoke to the girl whose name tag read Tyasia.

"I'm doing fine thank you for asking and I'll let Diamond know you're out here," she replied getting up from behind the desk.

I started tapping my foot on the floor while there were women walking past me with their noses turned up! Like there was dog shit on my shoe, I turned my nose up in response, and matched their nasty glares. Even with my natural hair up in a puff, I was still shutting shit down.

"Bitch why you looking all mean and shit like that," Diamond said walking up and giving me a hug.

"The fuck y'all looking at? Shoo shoo bitches," Diamond snapped.

I guess she caught the wandering stares of the women walking past as well.

"These hoes got the game all fucked up," Diamond vented.

"Tell me about it," I responded.

"But fuck them, this is my damn business and I will put their asses out in nothing but a robe and half of a cucumber face mask," she continued. I couldn't do anything but laugh.

"Girl, I'm glad you came when you did. I can't have my girl walking around like this." Diamond commented on my wild mane.

"Girl, that's why I asked you to squeeze me in. I've already washed and greased it, so all you have to do is braid it and then sew me up."

"Say no more, you already know I got you. I just got this Malaysian Deep Body Wave that'll look flawless on you. I'm about to hook you up, all I need to know is whether you want a side or middle part," Diamond rambled on.

"Middle part," I told her then leaned back for her to work her magic on my hair.

There is just something about getting my hair done that relaxes me, coupled with the fact that I love to look good at all times.

"Girl, look over there at her, why she looking like that."

"Look at her sitting over there all entitled, bitch you getting your hair done in the same place we are."

"I know right, girl you crazy." I overheard two females talking about somebody and high-fiving each other.

I didn't see how people could just be content hating on the next bitch. You get the same twenty-four hours as everybody else. Don't get mad at somebody for making good use of their time. I didn't want to listen to them bitches, but that was hard considering how loud they were talking. I couldn't see what they looked like, but I knew from the loud popping of bubble gum and the smacking of gums that they were probably gutter rats.

I sat up to pull out my phone and plug in my headphones. I'm not about to be sitting in here for a couple of hours listening to the cackling of these two hens. Instinctively my eyes roamed the room until they fell upon two girls who I assumed were the ones gossiping.

When our eyes met they were both staring directly at me. I broke eye contact first and got comfortable, so Diamond could really get started on my hair. There was no music playing yet because I was trying to find a good playlist on Pandora first.

"You see how she was staring at us? Girl, I will beat that bitch's ass," chick one said popping big shit.

"Bitch, you know you can't fight," Chick two clowned.

"Whatever hoe, I can't hate though Rich Money's girl is killing this dress on this red carpet, to be a big girl."

"She damn sure is, but I wonder what her man's dick is like. He looks like he's walking around with a third leg. Rich Money and Blake Mulah are doing a show here soon and word on the streets is that Rich doesn't mind bringing women from the crowd backstage, to his tour bus, or in his hotel room. Shit, if I play my cards right I just might be that lucky somebody," chick two told her friend.

It was at that moment that I realized those hoes was talking about me the entire time. When I looked over at them I saw one holding a magazine with a picture of me and Rich featured on the cover. I was about to pop up and give them bitches a piece of my mind, but something told me to wait, because the plot was about to thicken.

"You could never get lucky trying to fuck with Rich Money," a voice said that was different from the other two said.

"And why is that," chicks one and two said in unison.

"Because he already has a bitch," the random voice said.

By this time their conversation had drew the attention of the entire hair wing of the salon.

"We all know he has a bitch at home, but who cares, what she doesn't know won't hurt her," chick two said.

Figuring it's now my time to make my presence known I tapped Diamond so she could stop braiding my hair for a moment, but that was before a bomb was dropped that made the room fall silent.

"No, he's only with her for their kid. I'm with him the whole time he's on the road. I'm the bitch that fucks his brains out on a daily basis; the bitch he just bought and furnished a condo for, and the bitch that's about to have his baby. That is why you will never have a chance at fucking with him, because I already have that covered," the other girl stated matter-of-factly.

None of these hoes must have recognized me to know who the fuck I am, but I'm about take all of them to school.

"How cute is that? Y'all in here crushing over Rich Money," I laughed. The bird brains tucked their tails and shut up I guess they now knew that I was the one they referred to as "pretty for a big girl".

"This is far from a crush, boo. Rich is my man, the only reason we haven't gone public with our relationship yet is because he wants to protect his image and wait until his daughter is older so she won't think he just abandoned her. Trust me honey this is where he wants to be," the random girl said.

I took a good look at her before responding, I had to give credit where it is due. She is a pretty brown thing with mesmerizing green eyes. My eyes moved down to her stomach and she had a little pudge.

"Don't you think that if he really wanted to be with you that he wouldn't give a fuck about his image? A real man makes a way, he doesn't make excuses," I said to her.

I heard Diamond behind me whispering on the phone, but I wasn't paying her any mind.

"I know he loves me, so that's all that matters," she countered with her arms now folded snuggly across her chest.

"So what did he say about his baby mama at home?" I asked her. I had to have all necessary information before I read this hoe her rights.

"He said he doesn't really even want to be with her, but he doesn't want to drag his daughter through a nasty divorce by leaving her mother."

"Oh really," I replied with a look of bewilderment etched across my face, "Well let's find out for sure. What's your name?"

"Ebony," she replied.

She looked at me confused but I didn't care. I knew she was going to sit there and wait to see what I had to show her. I unplugged my headphones and threw them into my Celine bag. I called Rich on FaceTime.

"How you feeling baby?" I asked him.

"I could be better, but I can't complain," he said in sexy slow drawl.

"I just wanted to check on you, plus the ladies in the shop don't believe I'm the infamous Alani Clarke that is with new up and coming rap mogul Rich Money," I said with a sinister grin etched across my face.

I glanced over at the girl Ebony to gauge her reaction, but I couldn't read her face.

"Fuck them bitches, you don't have to prove shit to them, but if it'll make you feel better hold the phone up and show them hoes that I'm the nigga that gets to come home to your sexy ass every night that I'm not on the road," Rich responded.

Deciding that I wanted to be a petty Betty I did just that. I made sure to lag on Ebony so that Rich could see her and so that she could also see him.

"You lying ass bitch! You told me that you were leaving her!" Ebony snapped standing up.

"I'll talk to you later at the house babe. I got some shit to take care of here," I said hanging up the phone.

"You're not about to waste my unlimited minutes and data talking to a man that you seem to think is yours on my phone," I told Ebony watching her chest heave up and down, while tears streamed down her pretty face. She didn't even bother responding to me, she just stood there steaming mad.

"What's going on?" Khanna said bursting into the salon with Bam in tow looking like she was ready to kill a brick for no reason.

"Nothing at all, me and the ladies were just sitting here conversing," I replied sitting back, so that Diamond could finish my hair.

They must have been who Diamond was calling. I'm glad to know my girls have my back, but I can most definitely hold my own. I didn't need them coming to my rescue every time something went down, no matter how big or small the situation may have been.

"Well, since I'm here, I might as well get my shit touched up," Khanna stated taking a seat. "Can you squeeze me in, Diamond?"

"You know it, boo. I got you right after La'La's crazy ass," Diamond laughed.

"Shit, you might as well clear your damn schedule. Fucking with that damn Blake, my shit looking like a damn Brillo pad," Bam added and we all laughed.

Some of the women in the shop sucked their teeth while others rolled their eyes. Chick one grew some balls and spoke up, "We been sitting here waiting longer than all of them," she complained.

"And you're going to wait even longer or you can get the fuck out. Those are your only two options," Diamond raised her voice while pointing a comb in the girl's direction.

She didn't bother responding to Diamond, because she knew that she was dead ass serious, instead she sat back in her seat and rolled her beady little eyes up in her head.

I laughed and then spoke "And boo, I'm not pretty FOR a big girl, I'm pretty BECAUSE I'm a big girl."

I looked across the room after checking chick one and two and Ebony was still standing there crying looking pathetic.

"Girl, you're still here. I would have thought you had enough embarrassment for the day. You can come back tomorrow or later on when I'm not here to get your shit done," I said meaning every word.

I no longer had the desire to share air with the bitch who was fucking my man.

Ebony looked around the room and upon noticing all the eyes in the room were focused on her she quickly gathered her things and made a dash for the exit.

"Ebony wait up," I spoke to her departing back. She stopped just shy of the exit but, didn't bother to turn around.

"For the record, Rich and I are not married, I have a child, but my daughter is not for Rich, so we have no ties to each other really with the exception of fucking each other's brains out. Oh, I did just get divorced from the father of my child and he is the man who has had my heart and whom I should have been with from jump. Rich is all yours boo. I'll have him out of my house and into yours by the end of today. He might be a little banged up because I tied him up and beat his ass this morning, but I'm sure you will nurse him back to health."

"He and I have no ties to each other, so you will never have to worry about me. Have a good life with him and his STDs, I can definitely do without the headache," I said.

I usually am not one to have my business all in the streets and I know that is sure to happen talking in front of a salon full of nosey bitches, but I had to let her know what was up. She just continued to walk out and never looked back.

Rich and I are a thing of the past. If I left my husband the morning after our wedding for his infidelities, then he ought to have known that fucking around would end any relationship between us. I don't have time to be keeping niggas that didn't want to be kept. I'm too pretty and too much of a good person for that.

Kanye shrug. I was a fool for one nigga and I flat out refuse to play the dummy again. At the end of the day, I care about Rich a lot, but I don't love nor am I in love with him. The person that had my heart was the man who always had it.

Khan was the only man I loved and probably the only man I'll ever love unless I could shake the hold that he still seemed to have on me and my heart.

Chapter 36

Ebony

I walked outside of Heavenly Touch crying so hard that I started to make myself sick. I leaned over the side of my new Range Rover lurching up the entire contents of my stomach. Once I got in my car, I sat there for a moment trying to piece together my life.

It took everything in me to keep from crying in that shop full of women. To hear that Rich had been lying to me the entire time had me feeling as if I didn't know whether I was coming or going. I knew we met and got together upon questionable circumstances, but he had no reason to keep me in the dark about his real relationship with his baby mama or should I just say girlfriend.

To learn in front of everybody that the man I have been with, making life plans with, and having a baby with had no intention of leaving the woman he was with, was like shooting a dagger through my heart. They technically had no ties to each other, so he could have left her at any time and we could've been together.

Her daughter isn't his daughter, so he could have left a long time ago. Even though I felt that it was some foul shit that Rich had done to me, I took partial blame for it. I came on to him in his dressing room, like some random groupie hoe. But the truth was that I grew up with Rich and Blake. Blake used to tease me about being overweight and ugly, he used to push me and pull my hair. To make matters worse, I had severe allergies as a child, so my nose was always running.

Regardless of how many times Blake picked on me, Rich was the one to come check on me and make sure I was okay. If Blake tripped me, Rich would always be the one to help me up and brush off my skinned knees. One day asked him why he continued to hang with Blake when they were like day and night. All he said was that Blake was his nigga and his peoples looked out for him, so he had to look out for Blake in return and that he was more than a friend to him; that he was his brother.

I couldn't do anything but respect it. You could tell that he was the type of person to ride till the wheels fall off, get out, and put them back on for the people he loves. I loved that about him then and love it even more now.

Rich and Blake later moved away and we lost touch. We would chill from time to time when Blake wasn't around, until one day I didn't see them anymore. I would hear people talking about them ringing bells in these streets, but I never saw them. I swore to myself that when I saw Rich again, he wouldn't be able to slip through the cracks of my fingers again.

I grew up, lost weight, and went to a specialist to help with my allergies. When I caught wind of Rich and Blake blowing up, I made it my business to be at their show. The rest is history, but who would have ever though that Rich and Blake would switch places.

Blake seemed to be the perfect gentleman, he had a girl that to my knowledge he doesn't step out on. When I'm on the road with Rich, which is majority of the time, I've never seen Blake even look at another woman with lust-filled eyes. He would go straight back to his suite or the tour bus when the shows were over.

Rich on the other hand, partied hard and fucked multiple bitches. I joined him with some just to keep him happy. I didn't wait all these years for the man of my dreams only to let him slip through the cracks of my fingers, yet again. I didn't like women, but I did it to keep him happy. I figured sooner or later he would get the 'party like a rock star' mentality out of his system.

So I let him have his fun, but only with the promise of us making shit official in the near future. He told me as soon as his divorce was final it would be him, his daughter, and me. That lying ass nigga told me his "Baby Mama" was an unfit mother and that he couldn't leave his daughter with her.

I can't believe he straight lied to my face like that, but I'm even more disappointed in myself. I should have done better research on his ass. Shit, I could have googled his ass, to find out the information I needed to know.

Knowing that he heard and saw me on La'La's Facetime, I was half expecting my phone to ring, but I guess that was wishful thinking. Pulling myself together I dried my tears, refreshed my makeup, and drove off. Fuck Rich and the bitch he got his name from.

A bitch like me would never be down for too long. I may not have known my worth while growing up, but I damn sure knew it then. I was going to be good with or without Rich. You better believe that.

Chapter 37

Somaya

"Bitch you crazy as hell, I'm not about to play with you," I laughed at my cousin Lina. We were chilling in the living room of the house I share with Khan, shooting the breeze. He was gone to take his kids somewhere and had taken Somalia with him. I will forever be grateful for snagging a man like him. All his previous bitches had fucked up by letting him go, but I didn't plan to. Khan is the epitome of a good man and I'm glad that I found him.

He has since upgraded my life and Somalia's as well. She has been treated like the princess she is. She loves Khan like he's her real father and I love seeing him interacting with her and his biological children.

I took a sip of my wine cooler and sparked up a blunt. Khan wasn't here, so I didn't have to worry about him complaining about my slight drinking and smoking. A wine cooler here and there won't harm the baby that we were blessed with. I tried giving up cigarettes, but what can I say, I'm a work in progress.

"Girl, I'm serious, that nigga fucked me into a coma, bitch I was ready to go to the jewelry store, buy his ass a ring, and propose to his ass. His dick game is just that bomb," Lina said telling me about her sexcapdes.

"Girl, I don't care about your little sex sessions. I'm pretty sure your nigga ain't got shit on mine so I could care less."

I didn't have a problem with rubbing my new found love in bitch's faces. That was one of the perks of dating a boss and I was loving it.

"Bitch don't nobody give a fuck about you and your nigga," Lina added.

"And you think I give a fuck about yours," I countered with a slight attitude.

No bitch will ever get the pleasure of coming for my nigga and living to tell the story.

"Well excuse the fuck out of me. We have always shared stories about the men in our lives with each other. How the fuck was I supposed to know that shit is different now?" Lina snapped back with just as much sass as I had used on her.

She started grabbing her stuff preparing to leave. I could tell that she had an attitude, but I couldn't care less. Instead of being salty that bitch needed to be paying homage to me and Khan.

When he afforded me a new lifestyle he gave her a new one as well. I left Lina with all my old clothes; let her and her three bad ass kids move into my old place, because it was bigger and better than the shandy shack that she had been staying in; and gave her my old Dodge Caravan to get around in so she wouldn't have to take the bus or worry me for rides.

I can't stand an ole, ungrateful ass hoe, and that is exactly what Lina was acting like. But fuck her, I can guarantee you she'll need me before I need her broke ass. Lina was putting her shoes on when Khan walked through the door holding KJ in his arms and Somalia walking behind him holding Karizma's hand. She had just started walking and she was so cute and bow-legged.

Looking at her made me wonder what our baby was going to look like. I smiled at them ready to get up and greet my man with a kiss until, he decided to shit on my good mood.

"Why the fuck you in here sitting around chilling like this the fucking Taj Mahal," he snapped with his dreads swinging looking like a sexy ass Greek god.

"Don't worry, Khan. I was just leaving," Lina said walking past him and out of the door.

Just like her bitch ass to leave me to deal with his bipolar ass on my own.

"Somalia take the kids and put them in their rooms for a nap," Khan said looking like he was ready to tear me a new asshole.

Even though that look on his face didn't do anything but make my pussy wet and throb.

Khan watched as Somalia grabbed both of the kids and made her way to the back of the house. When he was sure that they were behind the closed doors of their rooms he proceeded to rip into me.

"What the fuck is wrong with your stupid ass? When I get home from doing anything, whether it's hugging the block or whatever, all I want is some warm pussy and a hot meal."

He stepped further into the room and his eyes changed colors.

"What the fuck is this?" he asked.

I watched him pick the half-smoked blunt I had put out up from the ashtray while I tried to think of a lie.

Before I could even utter a word, he smacked fire outta my ass. I reached my hand up to touch the spot on my face that he'd struck and it was warm to the touch.

"Khan, have you lost your damn…" That was all that I got out before I was grabbed by my hair and dragged towards the front door.

"Why the fuck you smoking and drinking while you pregnant with my damn seed?" he asked as he continued to drag me.

Damn, my doctor told me I could have a glass of wine here and there, so I didn't think drinking a wine cooler would have been that bad, nor did I expect Khan to react like this to finding out.

"Bitch, you can get the fuck out of my house, if this is how you're gonna act. If you don't give a damn about my child while it's still in your stomach, then I know you're not gonna give a fuck when it gets here. Being a mother starts now and you are already fucking up. You can come back when you learn how to be a mother and my woman," Khan snapped with his nostrils flaring and his dreads swinging back and forth.

He looked like a mad man and for the first time in our relationship I was actually scared of him. He continued to drag me by my hair while I kicked and screamed. I could feel chunks of my hair literally being ripped from out of my scalp. Khan threw me onto the front porch, closed the door, and locked it.

I took a few seconds to get myself together before I jumped up and started banging on the door.

"Khan! All I need is my purse and my daughter, until then I'm not leaving!" I screamed waiting for him to answer the door for me.

I'll leave his house, but I flat out refuse to leave without my daughter. Plus, I needed some money and my car keys, which was all in my purse.

"Here bitch catch an Uber. Somalia ain't going nowhere. You can't even take care of the child in your stomach, why would I feel safe to assume that you would take proper care of her. But don't worry she's in good hands," Khan said and closed the door back.

"Why can't I take my truck?" I asked him through the door.

"Because I bought it bitch that's why, plus you're ratchet ass is ungrateful."

I didn't even bother to respond. I knew he wouldn't let anything happen to my daughter. He treated her like she was his daughter and Somalia called him daddy.

Even though Khan just dragged my ass out of the house we share, the reason made me love him even more; it showed that he cared even though he tried his hardest to keep it under wraps. I loved Khan and I know he loved me, otherwise he wouldn't have done all of the things that he has done for me and Somalia. All I have to do is show him that I'm a great mother and and we will be good.

First things first, no more drinking and smoking for me. I'm going to go get a hotel room until Khan calms down. We are still new to this relationship thing and we did move kind of fast without properly getting to know one other, but I plan changing things around starting with myself.

Chapter 38

Rich

When I saw my Emerald Ebony in the background while I was on facetime with La'La, I damn near shitted on myself. I didn't think that I was going to have to explain my indiscretions this early in the game.

I called Alani's phone back repeatedly and each time I got no answer. I sat up in bed and tried to get up, but the pain from the wounds La'La inflicted caused me to pause. I popped two of the pills the hood doctor left for me on the nightstand, then got up.

I hopped in the shower and allowed the hot water to soothe the aches in my body. When I got out, I dried off and examined myself in the mirror. I was in dire need of a shave, but that would have to wait. I ran my hands across the wounds on my chest. They weren't as bad as I thought they would be, nothing I can't get a tattoo over. Some of them looked like they would heal completely on their own.

Walking back into the bedroom, I grabbed the clothes I wanted to wear for the day. Nothing extravagant, I needed to be comfortable. I threw some boxer briefs, a white tee, and some Nike joggers on the bed. I grabbed my phone from the nightstand and attempted to call La'La again, but I got no answer. I called back three more times and she still didn't answer the phone.

I had no clue how to get my girl back, if I hadn't lost her completely already. She had to have known that I was cheating or at least cheated once before, because of the STD I'd contracted and then passed onto her.

I don't know what Ebony told her; Alani could possibly know everything. I saw Ebony's pregnant belly clear as day through that Facetime call, so I know Alani and everybody in the shop, saw it as well. If Ebony told them that we are fucking, then I know Alani put two and two together and came to the conclusion that I'm that father of that girl's unborn baby.

I always expressed to Alani that I would treat her way better than her Ex did, but here I am making the same mistakes. When Ebony and I first learned of her pregnancy, I was ecstatic. The thought of being able to have a child that will bare my last name made me feel good.

I do everything that a father would do for their own daughter for Karizma and I call her my daughter, but the fact still remains that she isn't my daughter. Karizma belongs to Khan. Ebony's child belongs to me. It may be some fucked up logic, but whatever. That's why I didn't push Ebony to get an abortion.

At the same time, with her isn't where I want to be. I love and want to be with Alani. She just didn't want to have any more children until Karizma was older. I understood it, although it didn't change that fact that I wanted children of my own.

I filled Ebony up with false hope and promises of us being together one day, knowing good and damn well that I never had any plans on leaving Alani. I'm just a man who wants my cake and wants to eat it too. Is there any crime in that?

*****

I pulled up in front of Heavenly Touch and hopped out of the car. I didn't have a clue what the fuck I was going to tell my girl, but I was going to tell her something.

I had plans to call and check on Ebony later, at that present moment, I needed to have my number one team player back in the game. I hopped out of my car and headed towards the entrance. When I walked inside I received countless stares and heard the whispers of the thirsty females too shy to step to a boss nigga that's a celebrity.

I stepped up to the receptionist desk, "Yo ma, where is the hair section to this big ass salon?" I asked her.

"OMG, you.. you.. you're Rich Money! This might sound a little groupie-ish and you probably get this all the time, but can I take a picture with you?" the receptionist asked me.

The smile on her face coupled with how giddy she was acting made her look like a teenaged school girl.

"One picture," I told her sounding monotone. I didn't have time for this shit, but I took the selfie with her.

"Thank you so much, if I didn't take this picture nobody would believe me when I told them that I met Rich Money. Thank you again. The hair section is right that way," she pointed to her left and my right.

"Thanks ma," I responded and handed her a couple of C-notes.

I headed in the direction she pointed and could hear laughter behind the double doors labeled "Diamond's Salon," when someone walked out. I pushed the doors open and walked inside. It seemed as if all communication ceased once my presence was noticed.

I scanned the room and caught glimpses of Alani, Khanna, and Bam. The other women in the room all started whispering amongst themselves as I walked further inside. I headed in Alani's direction, she was in one of the six chairs getting her hair curled with some type of wand.

"Ma, let me holler at you real quick," I said to Alani while grabbing her hand.

"Rich don't you see me getting my damn hair done? I'll talk to you later on at the house while we're packing your shit," La'La snapped after snatching her hands back from my clutches.

I saw Bam grab her purse out of my peripheral, which led me to believe that she was itching to put a bullet in my ass.

"It'll just take a minute," I practically begged her.

"Whatever you have to say to me Richard you can say it right here."

I took that as my queue to do what I had been planning for months now. I dropped down to one knee, pulled out the velvet ring box I had in my pocket and took her hand in mine.

"Alani, I have never wanted anything more in life than to be your man, which is why I chased you and have never given you the chance to attempt to get away from me. I have always promised to treat you better than your last nigga, and I want to continue to make good on that promise for the rest of my life. With all that being said, will you make me the luckiest nigga in the world by taking my last name and bearing my kids?" I asked her.

I have been preparing to propose to her for a while now. I was going to do it at my next home show, but now is as good a time as any. I have to show her that even though I have a baby on the way with another bitch, she is still the most important woman in my life.

I was still down on one knee and every moment that passed that she didn't answer me felt like an eternity. I started to get up because I was feeling a little slighted. La'La was just sitting there and staring in my face. Before I could rise up fully, she started to speak.

"Rich, I thought I loved you, no scratch that I thought, I was in love with you, but I now realize that I was only in love with the thought of you. I was in love with the way you treated me. I loved how you catered to me, you knew how to make my body, mind, and soul feel good.

If I wasn't feeling well you would keep Karizma for me and take care of me until I felt better. When I was still hurting and crying over Khan, you were the one to dry my tears. You've stepped up to the plate and made sure my daughter has never wanted for anything, even when her biological father wasn't there for her.

She has always known what a father's unconditional love feels like thanks to you and I'll be forever grateful to you for that, but this façade of a relationship can go on no longer. You possess all of the qualities that I look for in a soul mate, but none of that negates the fact that you have a child on the way with another woman.

I was a fool for one man and I will not be one for another man. I've enjoyed the time we've had together, but sadly our time has expired. I'm still in love with another man, and even though I don't want to be, it's the sad truth. I wish I did love you, you were good for me, well at least you were until this happened.

Since I can't love you, I'll wish you the best on all of your future endeavors. I know you'll be a great father to your child because you were always one to Kay-Kay. I got mad love for you Rich, but have a nice life."

Each word she spoke sent a dagger through my heart. Instead of trying to plead my case in a room full of nosey women, I got up, brushed off my pants legs, kissed Alani on her forehead, placed the ring in her hand, and walked out. I chose to bow out gracefully instead of further complicating things by acting an ass.

As I neared the door I could already begin to hear the chatter of the ratchet women whom occupied the shop.

"Girl, I would have said yes and then hopped right on his dick!" One girl said.

"Damn right, if you don't want him I'll take his sexy ass."

I just continued to walk out the door and to my car. I shook my head at the realization that I had lost my down ass chick, fucking with a ditzy ass bitch. I couldn't dwell on it though because I know that it would consume my thoughts.

As an alternative to going to the home I once shared with La'La, I headed over to the condo I had purchased for Ebony. I only got it for her because I wanted to have somewhere to beat her pussy up when I was home and she wasn't on the road with me.

I pulled up to the condo and when I got to the door I used my key to turn the lock and open it. I got the shock of a lifetime when I realized that it had been cleaned out. It was spotless as if no one had ever even lived there. When she would have had the time to do any of this is beyond me. It has to be a new record or something for you to lose two women in the same day.

Chapter 39

Alani

If Rich thought that I was going to take his friendly dick ass back after learning of his infidelities, then he had the wrong chick. This was the new and improved La'La, gone were the days that I allow ANYBODY to walk all over me or do me dirty. What I don't understand is how he could even think we had another chance at being together, when he has a baby on the way with another broad.

I left Khan for the same shit and we were married, I have no ties to Rich, so I can leave him without so much as a second though. And what's up with these niggas thinking that a ring is supposed to change some shit. Khan fucked up, proposed to me, I said yes, we got married, we got divorced, we miss each other, and we're co-parenting.

Then I found out Rich has a love child on the way, same as Khan, then he comes in the shop trying to propose to a bitch. Boo-Boo the fool must be written across my forehead, because these niggas keep thinking I'm stupid.

I need to figure out what it is about my pussy that's attracting ain't shit niggas. I must be destined to an old cat lady with cob web pussy. It's time for me to take a step back and reevaluate my life. The only two men I have ever been with in my life have had outside children on me.

Diamond reached down and rubbed my shoulders. "It's gonna be okay, boo," she reassuringly stated.

Once Diamond finished up my hair, I went to the other side to get my nails and feet done while I waited on Khanna and Bam to finish. Afterwards, we made plans to hit up Happy Hour at CHIC. I definitely needed to unwind and get my thoughts together after that day's series of unfortunate events.

Chapter 40

Khanna

I sat up in bed breastfeeding Kadir, while repeatedly declining Dae's calls. He was pressing me to let him see Kadir, but I wasn't feeling that shit. He had the game fucked up. I just can't seem to comprehend why me and everybody around me is falling victim to their men having children with other women. Me, La'La, and Bam have all had to deal with this happening to us.

You may call me petty for not allowing Dae'Sean to see his child, but I don't give a damn. Kadir was a Thomas which means he was strong, Dae was a bitch for what he did, and I don't want any bitch ass niggas around my son. I don't care if he is his father. I can do bad all by my damn self. I damn sure don't need bummy ass Dae'Sean to assist me in taking care of my son.

Kadir and I had the same sleeping pattern, so he didn't keep me up at night. If I was hungry I knew he was hungry as well. My baby slept through the night for the most part; the only time he would wake up crying is when he was wet. He was just an all-around good baby and I loved to shower him with my love and affection.

"What!?!" I snapped once I answered the phone for Dae'Sean.

This is like his twentieth time calling this morning and it's only 10 o'clock.

"When are you gonna let me see my son Khanna? He is mine isn't he?" this nigga had the nerve to ask.

"Nope in fact he isn't yours," I replied and hung up the phone. I didn't have time to play these kid games with Dae'Sean. If he didn't believe that Kadir was his son, then I wouldn't force him to think so. If I never have to see Dae'Sean again it would be too soon.

Just as I laid Kadir down for his mid-morning nap, my phone chimed letting me know that I had just received a text message. I opened it and it was from Dae.

FuckBoy: If you don't willingly let me see my son, Im'ma just take you to court for custody.

Me: Police ass nigga, I'll beat your ass, try me bitch!

I don't have time to play with Dae'Sean and his community dick having ass. At the end of the day I'm Kadir's mother and I had the final say so and I get to choose who I want to have in my son's life.

Dae'Sean had me fucked up if he thought that either me or Kadir needed him in our lives. I was good before him and my son and I will be good without him.

Chapter 41

Khan

I drove to Alani's house to drop the kids off. Even though KJ and Kay-Kay's birthdays are like two weeks apart, they're so close in age I'd decided to throw their parties together. I wanted to reserve a park, but my mother insisted we have it at her house. Then I told her I would have the food catered so she wouldn't have to do anything, but she shut down that idea as well.

Megan claimed that she didn't want anybody pumping her grandbabies full of chemicals. She insisted so I stopped trying to argue with her. I just gave her money to buy the food and paid her two grand for cooking it. At first she said she didn't need to be compensated for cooking for her grandkids, but eventually she slid the money in her purse. It was either she took the money or I was going to deposit it in her account.

I hopped out the car and went around to let Somalia and Kay-Kay out. Somalia grabbed Kay-Kay's hand while I carried KJ. I led the way up to Alani's door and knocked once I made it.

"Hey mommy's baby, I missed you so much!" La'La squealed picking up Karizma and kissing her cheeks.

She held the door open for the rest of us to walk in. After she finished loving on Karizma, she grabbed KJ from my arms and kissed his cheeks as well.

"How are you Somalia?" she asked her, but Somalia just waved and hid behind my leg.

"Where's my kiss at?" I asked La'La.

Instead of protesting or talking shit like she usually does she puckered up her lips, stood on her tip toes, and planted a fat juicy kiss on my lips.

"There you go, are you happy now?" I just smiled at her, and instead of her waiting for me to answer she continued.

"Did you pack the kids and Somalia's clothes for the party?" she asked me.

"What kind of father do you think I am?" I jokingly asked and laughed.

"Just making sure," she commented and cut her eyes at me.

I needed to be on my way to make sure my children's party had everything in order, but I knew my mother was going to make sure it was straight, so I sat down, kicked my shoes off, and propped my feet up on the table.

"Umm, excuse me sir, why are your feet on my damn coffee table like you done lost yo' damn mind? Ain't shit changed with me with the exception of the day of the week," La'La snapped with her head cocked to the side and one hand perched perfectly on her hip.

"Girl, miss me what with that shit," I replied with my feet still on her table.

"Somalia, take the kids to the play room at the top of stairs while I make you guys some snacks," Alani's said and Somalia complied.

Not letting her get a chance to go in on me I asked her "Why all them boxes by the door?"

She may have thought I didn't, but I did notice all Rich's belongings packed up by the front door.

"Well…" she started and proceeded to tell me the story of what happened between her and Rich.

By the time she was done I felt like shit all over again. Every man that she comes across after me will be judged because of the shit I put her through. If I had never fucked up she wouldn't have fallen into the arms of another man, only to end up hurt again and in the same predicament.

I could tell that she was feeling a certain type of way so I pulled her into my lap.

"I never liked that nigga anyway," I said holding her close.

It may not have been what she wanted to hear, but it was the truth.

"Some friend you are you asshole!" Alani said playfully jabbing me in the chest.

She looked so sexy to me pouting with her full lips poked out. Leaning in, I covered her lips with mine and sucked her bottom, lip biting it gently. La'La pulled back and looked me deep in my eyes. I thought she was about to kick me out but instead she kissed me back with so much in intensity I grabbed her ass for support.

I pulled back long enough to pull my shirt over my head and then hers. I then unhooked her bra to free her perky breasts. I hungrily sucked each one so that the other wouldn't feel neglected. Even though I couldn't wait to get up in her guts I didn't want to risk the kids walking in on us.

So I picked Alani up and she wrapped her legs around my waist. I carried her up the stairs and to her guest room. I refuse to lay this dick on her in a bed she's fucked another nigga in.

I laid her down on the bed, but she popped back up only to release my belt and allow my pants to fall to ground. La'La hungrily sucked my dick into her warm wet mouth, quickly reminding me why I think sex with her is heaven on earth.

Alani deep throated my dick while jacking me off with her right hand and massaging my nuts with her left. There are not even enough words in the English dictionary to describe how good it felt. La'La thought she was doing something, so in one swift motion I flipped her around and removed her pants and panties so I could feast on her pussy. La'La had pussy so sweet I could eat it anytime of the day and it would taste as fresh as if she had just gotten out the shower.

Her legs started shaking so I knew I had her right where I wanted her until she tried to get up. I wrapped my muscular arms around her legs to hold her in place. "Argh," she screamed. When she creamed all over the place, I decided to let her go.

She got up and collapsed on the bed, but I wasn't through with her yet. "I know you not tapping out yet," I smirked at her. Instead of responding she got up and pushed me back onto the bed.

Alani straddled me placing her freshly pedicured feet on either side of me and easing her slippery treasure chest down the length of my pole.

She started bouncing up and down on me and winding her hips on my dick. I tried to grab her hips to make her slow down, but she slapped my hands away. La'La started going stupid on the dick bucking her hips.

My nut was nearing so I flipped her over and started tearing that kitty up. In the missionary position I could stare straight into her eyes. The feelings I've tried to suppress came rushing back to me.

Her eyes tell her soul and that she's still in love with me as well. Too bad I'm in a relationship or I'd try to get that old thing back.

"Bae, I'm cumming," La'La hoarsely moaned out.

"I'm right behind you," I replied bussing hard, because I've been backed up from not getting any pussy after putting Somaya out.

After laying down recuperating for about five minutes, I got up. I looked over and La'La was knocked out. So I redressed in silence, then went downstairs to grab my shirt. After pulling it over my head I went into the kid's playroom and they were all sleep as well, so I put them in their beds and kissed them.

I know I'll see them later, but at no point do I ever want my kid's to feel like no one loves them. Then I went back to the room Alani was in to let her know I was leaving. I kissed her forehead and sent her a text message that I was leaving since she wouldn't wake up.

I locked up and left my baby mama's house with a little extra pep in my step due to my balls feeling lighter. Now to head to my mama's house to make sure everything is straight with my kid's party.

***

"Where are my grand babies? How they gone be late to their own party? I told you to just leave them here with me Khan," my mother fussed.

"I didn't want to overwhelm you with them while you out here doing your thing. Kay-Kay little ass be getting into everything now that she's walking and KJ just be trying to put everything in his mouth. So La'La got them. She should be on her way, though," I told her and she just walked off.

The turnout for the party was phenomenal. I finally convinced my mother to let me buy her a new house, so her back yard sits on two and a half acres. It was just enough space to fit a pony ride, a waterslide, two moon bounces, a face painter, and the whole nine. I spared no expense when it came down to my kid's happiness.

I heard clapping and screaming coming from the entrance to the backyard so I adjusted Maya on my lap so I could get a better view. I saw it was La'La and the kids so I tapped Maya's leg for her to get up.

Kay-Kay and KJ looked so cute in their denim shirts, camo pants, and Jordan's. La'La and I made eye contact and she smiled. My mother came out and grabbed the kids, then La'La made her way towards me. Just as she stopped in front of me, I felt a set of hands wrap around my body from behind.

"Oh, hey La'La I didn't see you there," Maya said knowing La'La is what made her come over.

"My name is Alani to you hoe," La'La replied.

"Whatever, thanks for watching the kids though. Khan and I had a lot of making up to do," Maya clapped back while discreetly grabbing my dick.

"Oh, is that right? So did this happen before or after he sucked and fucked the lining out my pussy? Oh, I should have figured that you didn't know, well anyways, y'all have fun. I'm off to go find my child and actually be a mother," La'La clipped, slid her shades on her face and walked off.

When I told La'La the shit that was going on with Maya, I didn't expect her to use it as ammunition, but oh well, Maya ain't going nowhere and she has let that be known on numerous occasions.

"Don't nobody give a fuck bitch! I'm still gone be with him!" Somaya yelled at Alani's parting back.

La'La didn't even bother to turn around.

"Why you keep fucking with that bitch like we don't have a baby on the way?" Maya turned and asked me.

"Because I'm a grown ass man that does what and who the fuck he wants," I stated then started to walk away.

"Oh and the way her pussy still fits this dick like a glove, I'll probably never leave her alone," I added and walked away completely.

La'La still got some Grade A pussy even after pushing out my seed, so I already know I'm going to hit that shit whenever I get a chance. She most likely won't let me after seeing me with Maya, but

I'll still try my hand. Alani got that snapper shit that just keeps me coming back.

I headed to go find my first baby mama and just when I spotted her Khanna stepped into my view.

"You can't speak," she asked with her hand on her hip. I was so sick of the women in my life thinking they hold any weight and they can try to thug me.

"Naw, I can't," I said and stepped around her.

"Where you going?" I asked Alani when I caught up to her.

"Away from here, I'll be back to get my daughter when her party is over" Alani said.

"Why would you leave when they haven't even sung happy birthday yet?" I asked her holding onto her arm loosely.

"I just have to go Khan, I'll be back later to get Kay-Kay," she said then looked away. It was then that I noticed the dried tear stains causing streaks in her foundation.

"Why are you crying?" I asked her concerned.

"Like you care," she countered attempting to walk away.

"Not until you tell me what's up."

"Okay, since you asked, you come to my house fuck me and then leave, only for me to come to my child's party and see you with your bitch," she said while tears just streamed down her face.

In my attempt to wipe them away more tears just fell to replace them. I didn't want to say it knowing the state she was in, but I couldn't hold it back.

"But were not even together, so I'm not understanding why you're even upset," I told her.

"You don't get it and you probably never will," she said.

"Help me to understand then," I told her.

"Just let me go Khan," she responded looking defeated.

The eyes of the woman I was staring at were empty and the realization hit me like a ton of bricks, Alani was only an empty shell of the woman she once was. The glow that she used to possess had dimmed. Although she was still beautiful, she had dark circles around her eyes and the wear and tear I had been putting on her heart was starting to show.

"I don't want to," I replied.

I couldn't imagine being without her even though we technically weren't together.

"Let me go Khan, you aren't doing anything but hurting me," she said with pleading eyes.

I looked down and noticed that I unknowingly had a tight grip on her arm and it was turning red. Although I know that wasn't the type of pain that she was talking about.

For some reason, I felt like this was our final goodbye.

Chapter 42

Alani

Khan had me fucked up in so many different types of ways. But at the end of the day, he was not the only one to blame. Once again, I had fallen for his charm and let him in, for a moment it felt like we were friends again. He came in when I was vulnerable after leaving Rich and I let him in.

When I saw him talking and chilling with his bitch at my daughter's birthday party, while I was watching her daughter, I almost lost it, but I'll never let a bitch see me sweat. I tried to leave only for Khan come talk to me. I didn't want to cry, but the tears came like water works.

I know I'm a strong person, but sometimes that's my downfall. When you're a strong person, no one stops to ask if you're okay. I left my daughter's party with a heavy heart. The only man I have ever loved had broken my heart, yet again.

I was so secure in myself that I just knew leaving Rich would mean that Khan and I would get back together. He had always had my heart and I felt as if he had learned his lesson, considering all that we've been through since we broke up.

Only to find out he just wanted to get some pussy and go back to his girl. Even though it pained me to see them together, after the time we shared earlier in the day, it was something that I needed to see. It showed me that Khan hadn't changed one bit. He was still the same nigga that fucked me over and played with my heart, feelings, and emotions time and time again. If I had expressed my thoughts on us getting back together I would have fallen down the same rabbit hole, but this time around I most likely wouldn't have found a way out.

I felt like a broken woman, like I was only a fraction of the person that I used to be. I just needed to take a step back from life and reevaluate all the decisions I'd made in life.

I needed to rekindle the flame that used to burn inside of me that had dimmed to only a flicker. Until then, I wasn't going to be any good to anybody not even my beautiful daughter, Karizma. I didn't want her to grow up and see how I've let her father treat me and think that's how she's supposed to be treated.

I was raising a Princess who will grow to be a beautiful queen one day. I wanted her to always know that she's priceless, and that she should never settle for less than she deserves. Before I can show my daughter what a strong woman looks like, I have to become the epitome of a strong woman.

I started to head to the home I once shared with Rich, so I could be alone with my thoughts before going back to pick up Karizma; but instead I made a detour and hopped on I-95 South with no set destination in mind.

Chapter 43

Khanna

That punk bitch Dae'Sean really took me to court for custody of Kadir. After laying Kadir down for a nap, I poured a drink of Apple Ciroc and sparked up a fat Kush blunt.

I turned on the baby monitor to ensure I would know when my pride and joy woke up. I had that state of the art shit that had a camera showing live footage of my baby. It even had an app that you could pull up on your phone. It was one of many gifts Alani got for me at my gender reveal party.

I just sat back smoking my blunt, but I couldn't stop looking at the Juvenile and Domestic court papers that had been served to me earlier this morning. This lame ass nigga actually had the audacity to ask for a paternity test and if Kadir turned out to be his, which I know he will, he wanted full custody.

Even after I finished smoking my jay and swallowed the last drop of my drink, I continued to stare at the certified documents in disbelief, plotting different ways that I could kill him and get away with it.

I mean I would have let him see Kadir eventually, when I was done being petty, but I just don't feel like being the bigger woman in this situation. If he cared about me or Kadir he wouldn't have slept with my EX best friend and gotten her pregnant with a baby everybody was under the impression was my brother's. I would've been a dumb bitch to be sitting around playing step mommy to a kid that was supposed to be my nephew.

Nobody that walks the face of this earth is going to take my son away from me. If he really cared about me and Kadir he would just leave us alone. He can just play house with Brooke and her son and just stop trying to take mine. Hell will freeze over twice before I allow Kadir to live with Dae'Sean and Brooke's loose pussy ass.

*****

My attitude was on ten. Pissed off is not even the phrase to describe the way I was feeling right then. That fact that I had to drag my son down to a DNA testing lab has me seeing red. If that shit wasn't court ordered, on everything I love, I wouldn't of have been there right then. The last thing I needed was to be locked up for a failure to appear and have to chance being away from my son.

On top of that, Dae'Sean would just use that as ammunition in court and try to deem me unfit. So there I was holding my crying child as a nurse swabbed his mouth, all because his daddy was a hoe ass nigga.

After the lady was done, I packed my baby up and headed out. He has been subjected to enough torture for one day. Walking out the door I bumped into none other than Dae'Sean and his lil Thotianna Brooke. Brooke's ole scary ass hid behind Dae'Sean like I was really going to do something to her while I had my son with me.

"Well look at this shit here, don't yall look cute," I said sarcastically.

"You should know how it feels to be without your child Brooke seeing as how you haven't seen KJ oh, I mean DJ, in months. But yet you stand here aiding him in trying to take my son away from me, whom he doesn't even care about. Because if he did he wouldn't have done his mother so dirty, but you know what they say stupid is as stupid does," I said walking out.

"Tell your brother I'm coming for my son too."

I didn't even bother responding to Dae'Sean and his empty threats, but I threw over my shoulder to Brooke.

"Watch your back Brooke you know what they say. The same way you get em' is the way you might lose em'."

Chapter 44

Ebony

After finding out that Rich fed me a bunch of lies, I fled the state. He was the only thing keeping me there. The Seven Cities of Virginia held nothing but bad memories for me, so I left and moved to Georgia without leaving so much as a contact address or a buddy list. It was just me and my baby starting over fresh.

I saved the majority of the money Rich had ever given me. I knew one day it was going to rain so I made sure I had an umbrella. I was taught to never put all of my eggs in one basket.

I stood in front of my full length mirror and couldn't help but stare at my round and protruding belly. I couldn't believe that I had a life growing inside of me, a human being that was created in love. Well at least it was love on my part.

Rich left a bruise on my heart when I found out the truth that was hidden behind his lies. I couldn't help but wonder if there was something that I did wrong. He was so loving and attentive; I still find it hard to believe he was so deceptive. Boy did he have me fooled.

In life you can't dwell on the mistakes of others, you just had to play the cards life dealt. I got a new phone and new number, but I still held onto my old one. Rich continued to call me every day, but I refused to answer the phone for him. I just kept the bill paid for that phone, because I smile a little bit knowing that he cared enough to call. Who knew, maybe one day I would come around once he got his life together and priorities in order and we could be a family.

*****

A knock on my door startled me, because I didn't know anybody in this city let alone this neighborhood. I looked through the peephole and saw that someone was covering it with their hand. Against my better judgment I opened the door and my heart stopped beating in my chest.

Rich was standing on the other side of my threshold looking dapper as hell in his Brooks Brothers suit and Roberto Cavalli shoes. His cologne greeted me with open arms and the feelings that I had for this man that I had been trying to suppress, came rushing back to me in tidal waves.

My kitty creamed at the sight of him. I wanted to say something, but I couldn't find the words. When I did find the words, they were caught in my throat. The saying cat got cha tongue rung true, because it sure had mine.

"So, this what I have do to talk to you?" Rich asked me leaning against the door frame.

I still couldn't formulate any words to respond to him so I just stood there staring at him. He just brushed past me and walked into the house taking a seat on my leather sectional.

Rich grabbed a framed ultrasound picture off of the coffee table and started examining it.

"Have you found out what you're having yet?" he asked me in an even tone.

Instead of answering his question I had a few questions of my own.

"What are you doing here and how did you find me?" I asked him straight up.

"Do you really think it was that hard? I've known where you were for a while now. I was waiting to see if you were going to stop being childish. You kept your other phone on in hopes I would call you, but I'm smart enough to know that you have another phone. But good thing you kept the other one on otherwise I wouldn't have been able to track you down. Now again I'm going to ask you, have you found out what we are having yet?"

"No not yet, I go back to the doctor to find out next week," was my only reply. He sure knew how to shut a bitch up.

Chapter 45

Rock

Things were a little rough adjusting to being a new dad, but I think I had the hang of things for the most part. It was just hard holding court in the streets, taking care of my daughter, and keeping up with Margo's demanding attitude.

This girl just might've been worse than Bam. With Bam, I could attempt to get around her acting crazy, but with Margo I couldn't do anything but take it because I never knew what was going to set her off. One minute she'd be all loving, the next she was trying to throw a vase at my head. I woke up one day to this crazy chick holding a gun to my daughter's head claiming that I loved Josiana more than I loved her.

That was the last straw for me. I took her to see a psychiatrist and they diagnosed her with postpartum depression and labeled her manic depressive. I had her admitted to a program so she could get better. If that bitch had killed my daughter she would have been getting buried right beside her. It was just me taking care of Josiana, but I still had an empire to build alongside Khan. I'd been getting Khanna and my aunt to watch my shorty for me when I was out handling business.

I'd also been avoiding Bam at all the traps because I didn't want to face her. The only thing I saw when I looked at her was her letting another nigga sample my goods. I know we ain't together, but she's still my bitch. Khan may have been able to sit back and watch his wife be with another man, but that shit ain't in me.

I knew if I saw Bam I would be ready to knock her head smooth off her fucking shoulders. I love her little ass too much to set my feelings aside so that she can be happy. I'm the only nigga she needs to be happy with.

*****

After dropping Josiana off with Khanna, I went to our main trap. The one we make the most money out of. And the first person I saw when I walked through the door was Bam. I spoke to my lil niggas and was going to walk straight past her until I noticed that she was sitting in that pussy ass nigga Blake's lap.

"What the fuck you got this pussy ass nigga in here for?" I asked her.

"Last time I checked, I ran this trap. And y'all niggas bring bitches up in here twenty-four seven, but when I bring a nigga up in here you got a fucking problem!" Bam snapped.

"You damn right I got a problem with it. I don't trust this fuck nigga!"

"Well, I suggest you get the fuck over it, because he's not going anywhere," she stated matter-of-factly then kissed his lips.

That nigga just sat there smiling happy as a lark, but that shit was about to be short lived. I walked over to where they were sitting and pushed Bam's little ass off his lap. I grabbed that nigga by his shirt and pulled him towards the door. Lil Speedy, one of my top workers, opened the door and I pushed that nigga out onto the porch, then slammed, and locked the door.

I turned around only to get nipped in my head by a Ciroc bottle that Bam threw. A runner by the name of Banks was holding her back and trying to calm her down while she shouted obscenities in my direction.

"Don't bring that nigga back in here, he can't even protect your stupid ass," I said then walked to the back.

I didn't have time to be fooling with Bam and her new flame. Now I was going to have to change the location of the Trap house I made the most money out of because she wanted to bring outside niggas into our circle, just because he was putting a little bit of dick in her life. I seriously didn't trust that nigga.

Chapter 46

Bam

Rock had some fucking nerve trying to throw Blake out on his ass. Niggas kill me, they can fuck whomever they want, but let you pop your pussy for just one other nigga and they would swear up and down you were the thot of the century.

I knew he could possibly be salty about walking in and seeing me getting my pussy ate like a box of Captain Crunch, but shit he should have called first before just popping up at my house, hell he could have at least knocked.

Fuck Rock, Blake and I had been great. He was everything I've ever wanted in a man. Although nothing in this world could replace my son, Blake had been doing an awesome job at patching up my heart. He paid great attention to me and I just enjoyed loving on him.

I just hated when he had to leave to go handle business. He traveled all over the states doing bookings, going to meetings, hosting parties, and the whole nine. We hadn't gone public with our relationship yet because the paparazzi be lurking and I was too deep in the streets to have somebody sneaking around behind me just to take a picture of Blake Mulah's girlfriend.

For the time being, I was perfectly content with the way our relationship was going. I was just basking in the glory of being loved on by such a beautiful man.

Chapter 47

Alani

I was lying on the beach of Fort Lauderdale, rocking a two piece high-waisted bathing suit, oversized Chanel shades, and an oversized sun hat; sipping on a virgin margarita, wishing I could have something stronger.

If you guessed that I was pregnant, then you guessed right. There I was again, pregnant by a man that had a baby on the way with another woman. If the tabloids caught wind of me being pregnant with Rich's baby at the same time as his mistress, they would have a field day with this news.

Good thing I've tried to keep my face out of the media as much as possible, I thought.

"I just love this salty air," Markita aka Mrs. Fitz commented, sipping her Patron margarita.

I called her after leaving my daughter's birthday party for an unbiased ear and shoulder to cry on. Next thing I knew we were taking a road trip down Florida. I called Khan before I made my abrupt departure to tell him that I just needed some time away to get my mind right, but of course he didn't answer the phone. I left him a voicemail, but he never responded. I tried calling him to talk to my Kay-Kay, but he never answers any of my calls.

In fact, I hadn't heard from any of my family since I'd been gone. But I just had to focus on me for a moment. I knew my daughter was in good hands with Khan and his family.

"That makes two of us," I responded.

Markita had helped me so much, especially with my divorce from Khan. She was just like having another mother figure in my life. The only difference was that she was a lot more laid back than my mother and Mama Megan.

"What's troubling you dear?" Markita asked me.

"What's wrong with me? Why does every relationship I've ever been in fail due to infidelities? What is it about me that lets these men think they can just fuck whoever they want and I'll still be with them? Rich and Khan, claimed to love me, but decided to shit on me. I must be a weak bitch people can walk all over."

"No, you're not weak at all. It takes a strong person to remove themselves from a toxic situation which you did with both men. You may not notice it, but deep down inside you know your worth, and that is the reason you didn't settle for half a man. Baby, you're stronger than you give yourself credit for, stop beating yourself up. For now, we will enjoy our time in the Sunshine State. We'll have to return home soon. You can't run from your problems, you have to put on your big girl panties and face your problems head on."

I was listening to what she was saying, but I wasn't trying to hear it. I was going to stay in Florida until I was ready to go home and not a minute before.

Chapter 48

Khan

It had been months since anybody had seen or heard from La'La. I knew that I had hurt her, but for her to just abandon her child on her birthday was just plain old fucked up. Karizma had been living with me and Somaya since Kay-Kay and KJ's party. But since Maya was about to have the baby it had been hard for her to move around, so I had been getting my mother to help out. Being a full time father and a full time go getter was tough, but real niggas don't fold.

Alani leaving without contacting anybody had me thirty-eight hot at first, but I eventually said fuck it. Just like I take care of Somaya's daughter, she helps me take care of mine. If Alani ever comes back she doesn't have to ever worry about seeing Kay-Kay again and I put that on my life.

***

I was sitting at the head of the table in the warehouse I use to conduct meetings smoking a blunt with Rock to my Right and my little cousin Chino to my left. For ten minutes I had been staring all the people that work for me in their faces daring a nigga to speak up and say something.

"Yo, Boss Man, what you got us here for? It's money to be made out here in these streets," Zay one of my runners asked.

I just stared in his direction until a bullet was fired entering his skull splattering brain matter on Mont and Lil Speedy who was sitting beside him. I didn't have to look to know that Chino was the one to deliver that bullet ending his life.

"He was a rat," I spoke calmly. "I have been losing money little by little for the past two months. I opted not to speak on it until I knew for sure who it was. Mont and Speedy, y'all are being promoted again. In fact, everybody is getting promoted except you, Dion."

I smashed my blunt in the ashtray and threw back my shot of D'usse.

"Why the fuck everybody getting promoted but me? I put in work just like the rest of these niggas! I got kids to feed!" Dion snapped

"And now she will be fatherless," I said delivering a bullet to his skull that ceased his existence.

"Mont and Speedy, y'all will be running your own traps from here on out. Chino, I'm opening new traps that I will need you to oversee. You will also be in charge of pickups and drop offs. Rock and I have more pressing matters, so Chino is who you all will be reporting to. I'm leaving things in the hands of Chino, so he is who y'all need to see if you have any problems. If y'all don't have any questions, you're dismissed."

I didn't care how anybody felt about me leaving my cousin in charge of things. Chino was family, so of course I was going to look out for him by making sure he ate. Chino's mother, Tanya, who is my mother's sister moved down to North Carolina once her husband, Chino's father, died in an attempt to get a fresh start.

I missed my lil nigga the entire time he was gone so when he got back, we were something like the three amigos. He was thugging it out with me when we were just some little niggas on a come up, so it was only right for me to show him my gratitude by putting him on.

***

I was speeding home trying to make it to Somaya. She called me telling me that she was having contractions. At first I thought it was just Braxton Hicks because she isn't due for another month until she said her water broke. She was crying and scared because she was the only one home with the kids.

I had made it to my house in record time making a mad dash for the front door. I didn't even bother turning my car off or closing the driver's side door. When I walked inside Somaya was standing by the front door with her hospital bag crouched over in pain.

"Let's go Khan. The kids are sleep and your mother is on her way over to keep an eye on them."

I helped her out to the car and got her situated just as my mother was pulling up. She got out of her car and walked over to me.

"Call me when the baby is born so that we can get a DNA test done."

"Come on Ma, not now!" I snapped. I kissed my mother on the cheek and walked off. I knew she meant well, but sometimes I just wish she didn't always say the first thing that comes to her mind.

I got in the car and Somaya screamed out in pain. "Hold on baby, we'll be there in no time."

I wasn't there for the moments leading up to the birth of either of my children so I really didn't know what to do, but I did know that I had to get my lady to the hospital so that she could deliver my baby healthy.

Doing eighty MPH helped me in getting to the hospital in record time.

"Baby, I think the baby is coming," Somaya groaned and I jumped out the car to get help.

When I made it back with a nurse and a wheelchair, Somaya was holding my baby in her arms trying to clean its mouth out.

"It's a girl," Somaya said.

I walked over to get a good look at my newest addition.

"I still feel like I have to push!"

"That's just the afterbirth. Sir, could you step out of the way for me?" The nurse asked and I obliged.

"I have to push, it feels like I need to push!"

Somaya started grunting and cries filled the air. I tried to get a good look at what was going on, but was bombarded by a whole slew of doctors. When they got Maya in a wheelchair my heart swelled ten times its normal size with joy.

"The second one was a boy. Baby, we have twins!" Somaya said cradling both of our kids in her arms.

Instead of following them into the hospital while they cleaned and stitched her up, I called up my entire family. This was a joyous occasion and who better to spend it with than the ones I hold near and dear.

***

Kameron and Kaarina we're born weighing six pounds two ounces a piece. *Who would have known that I popped twins off in Somaya's ass?* The doctor's didn't even see twins on any of her ultrasound's

"Thank you, Maya," I told her kissing her forehead.

"For what?"

"For giving birth to my big head ass kids," I laughed.

"Boy you're crazy."

"But check me out though, I have to go handle some business real quick. I'm going to take the kids to the nursery. I want you to get some rest."

Instead of protesting like I thought she would have she kissed me and laid back. As I walked out the room I ran right into my mom.

"Congrats son, they're yours."

She slapped some papers into my hands and then walked off. I looked at the papers and shook my head. My mother had gotten my kids tested that quickly. How she got my DNA to compare to theirs was beyond me. I didn't even know why she tested them, I told her they were mine from the jump.

Chapter 49

Somaya

There was no better feeling in this world than the feeling of euphoria that had me wrapped in a whirlwind the moment I gave birth to my twins. I had the same feeling when I gave birth to Somalia, but the difference is I had no one to share it with then. The fact that I have had Khan with me every step of the way has made this transition in my life that much easier. He has always been very much involved during my pregnancy, for that I am forever grateful.

Somalia's father had been absent for the better part of her life and now he's locked up on some gun charges, so he couldn't be in her life even if he wanted to. I refused to take her to go see him because that isn't the life I wanted for my daughter. I write him occasionally and keep money on my phone so that he can call and talk to her if he wants to. I even told him that he could be in her life when he touched down if that's what he chose.

I wasn't going to beg him to be in the life of a child we created together. Somalia and I were good without him and were even better now that Khan and I are together. He treats Somalia like she's his own and as far as she's concerned, Khan is her father. That man treats my daughter as no less than his own. Khan is God sent and any bitch that had let him slip through their fingers was a damn fool.

Fuck all that other shit though, Khan is my man now and I never plan on letting his ass go.

***

Finally, I got to leave the hospital with my babies in tow. I was being wheeled out of the hospital in a wheelchair, with Kaarina in her car seat on my lap, while Kane followed behind me holding Kameron. Khan pulled up at the entrance to the hospital as we made it outside.

Once we got the babies secured, we were on our way. Khan was looking good as fuck in his True Religion fit. His Creed cologne assaulted my nostrils and I wanted nothing more than to jump his bones. Unfortunately, I would have to wait six weeks for all that.

"Baby, where are we going? The house is in the opposite direction?"

"Don't ask me no questions," Khan stated flatly.

"I don't know who the fuck pissed in your damn frosted flakes this morning, but it damn sure wasn't me so you need to fix your attitude!" I snapped back at his ass.

He didn't even bother responding to me, but he had managed to piss me off that damn quick. Me raising my voice had startled the twins so I leaned over to tend to them. Just as I had got them quiet and was about to turn back around in my seat, we were rammed head on.

My first instinct was to protect my children, but another car hit us on my side on the car pushing us into oncoming traffic.

Khan's Benz was hit so many times, but the eighteen-wheeler hitting us caused us to flip. I don't know how many times my head banged against the window before my brain had enough and I passed out.

Chapter 50

Kane

After helping my son get squared away with the newest additions to the Thomas clan, I headed home to Megan. I just wanted be with her all of the time. I had been ripping and running all around town helping Khan get this family's situation together for the better part of the day.

Now I wanted nothing more than to take a shower, smoke a fat blunt, sip on some Hennessey, and fuck the lining out of Megan's pussy. The only thing that was standing in my way was this traffic that wouldn't let me be great.

I got out of my car to see what all the commotion was about. There was multiple car pile-up holding up traffic. I walked over to see how long it would take for them to clear it up. Megan had just sent some nudes to my phone and couldn't wait to make it home to her so that I could see the real thing.

When I made it to the heart of the madness, two EMT's were carrying away two car seats similar to the ones I just bought for my grandkids. I looked over at the car with the most damaged and it was the Benz that Khan was driving.

"Sir, you can't go over there," a Firefighter stopped me.

"Those are my grandchildren! They're only a few days old!"

When they finally let me through I ran to check on my grandkids first. They looked virtually unscathed.

"Sir you are very lucky! If it wasn't for these state of the art car seats they were in this could have been all bad. Unfortunately, their parents weren't so lucky."

In that instant, I had forgotten that my son was in possible peril. I watched in horror as they used the Jaws of Life to get Khan and Somaya out of the totaled car. My feet were frozen in place as I watched them rush them away. At least we were right by the hospital.

*****

I hated to make that dreadful call to my family letting them know that tragedy had struck us yet again. The doctors still hadn't come out so I didn't know what condition Khan was in.

Just as I put my head in my hands I heard Megan call out my name. Standing behind her was everyone we hold near and dear, we had taken over the hospital's waiting room. Regardless of what beef we have with each other we always manage to come together in a time of need.

*****

The doctor came out to deliver devastating news. Somaya was awake, but delirious, and they were keeping her sedated until her brain healed. Khan on the other hand was in a coma. He had two broken femurs, a broken arm, and a fractured cheek bone.

The doctors weren't optimistic about his condition, so I decided to get him moved home. *Why would I have people that didn't even believe he was going to pull through caring for him when he could be in the same house as his family?*

"I called Alani, but her number has been disconnected," Megan said, sitting down beside me and laying her head on my shoulder. I knew she was hurting and the only reason there weren't any tears sliding down her cheeks is because she was all cried out.

Megan cried so hard that she started hyperventilating and had to be admitted. Once I got Khan situated, I packed my family up along with the twins and headed home. It had been a long day and I wanted nothing more than to lie down and fall into a deep and peaceful slumber.

If the lord was willing I would wake up and this would have all been a disastrous nightmare.

Chapter 51

Megan

It seemed as if my family could never catch a break. Every time I turned around there was some bullshit lurking in the cosmos trying to bring harm to the people I hold near and dear to my heart.

I hired a team of nurses to care for my only son around the clock. His being in a vegetable like state was devastating. To keep my peace of mind and last little bit of sanity, I tried to think of it as him needing a break.

Khan was the head of this family and all he did was make sure we were all okay. He had been taking care of me and his sister for as long as I could remember. Since he was old enough to go out and make money on his own he had made it his business to make sure his sister and I were straight. No mother wanted her son to be out there in the streets for fear of him dying prematurely, but my hands were tied.

Khan had always been hard-headed and was going to do whatever he set his mind to. I'd told him on numerous occasions that I didn't need any of his money. Kane ensured that I would never have to work a day in my life if I didn't want to.

The pain that he put my heart through assisted me in my decision making process. I accepted his guilt money and made sure I provided the kids he abandoned with the best possible life I could give them. Khan just hated to see me doing everything. He was the man of the house and in his young eyes he was supposed to be providing for us and provide he did.

When Khan got a nice little stock pile he moved us up and out of the hood. My son has always gone hard for his family and he loves even harder. It was time that he rested and allowed us to take care of him. Only the Lord knows where we would be if it wasn't for Khan.

*****

I walked into the room that had been set up like a hospital room to check on my baby boy. Hood Doctor comes to check his vitals every four hours, but his nurses are here around the clock.

"Bitch, have you lost your fucking mind!" I snapped.

This little smut ass bitch was sucking my son's dick while playing in her funky ass pussy. Khan's dick came out of her mouth with a pop and was sticking straight up in the air.

"You nasty little necrophilia loving ass bitch, if you don't get your shit and get the fuck out of my house I'm going to be forced to put a bullet in your ass!"

That nasty little bitch hurriedly grabbed her things and ran from the room. She didn't even bother putting her pants back on, not that I would have allowed her to anyways. I made a call to Hood Doctor letting him know that his nurses were no longer needed.

I didn't know what kind of bitches he had under his supervision, but sucking the dick of a comatose man was unacceptable. Fuck that, that shit is flat out disgusting.

I still find it so hard to believe that women want to be with my son so badly that they'll do anything to get with him or just to say they had a sexual encounter with him. It is a crying shame when you aspire to have a claim to fame as being a wham, bam, thank you ma'am, to the king of the city. Khan's penis must be molded from gold to have all these girls going bananas over his ass.

I grabbed a bucket and some soap so that could rid my baby boy's body of his ex-nurse's DNA. I would be caring for him in between visits from Hood Doctor. After I got him cleaned up I went to grab products to retwist his dreads. Coma or no coma I couldn't have my baby walking around with his hair looking all crazy.

As he got older he stopped letting me do it, but I used to be the only person he trusted enough to touch his hair. I walked past the room I had turned into a nursery for the kids. I hit an about-face and walked inside to check on them. They were such good and quiet babies that I often forgot they were around.

After making sure they were still breathing and had dry pampers I prepared them each a bottle for when they woke up. Before I could make my way back to Khan I was interrupted by the ringing of my doorbell.

I pulled up the security footage and saw it was Somaya. She had discharged herself from the hospital completely disregarding the Doctor's orders upon her waking from her medically induced coma. But what I found strange is that she was just now making her way to my house even though it had been days since she left the hospital.

I made it my business to ensure that she was aware of me having my grandchildren while she and Khan were out of commission. I didn't want her to wake up panicking wondering where her newborns were.

"What do you want Somaya?" I asked through the intercom not opening the door.

"I came to see Khan he's not answering any of my calls or responding to my texts," she responded. I sighed but I still opened the door.

Maybe she's still out of it from the accident, I thought.

When I opened the door the reason behind my son's dumb ass baby mama acting like she got selective amnesia and forgot Khan was in a coma became evident. This hoe was on my doorstep pissy drunk at five o'clock in the afternoon.

"Somaya, if you don't get your stanking ass off of my doorstep I'm going to smack fire out of your dumb ass! You bitches got me fucked up today," I snapped.

"Bitches?! I know Khan ain't up in here with a bitch."

Somaya tried to push pass me into the house, but I blocked her. "Somaya your fucking children are upstairs get yourself together," I seethed in her ear.

"Oh no, I know that nigga ain't got some bitch around my kids!"

WHAP!

"Somaya, take your funky ass home, wash your ass, and go to bed! Sleep this shit off, you won't see your children until you do. Now get the fuck off my doorstep!"

I pushed Somaya off my porch making her fall into the flower bed. I didn't even bother to help her up. I just closed the door, locked it, and tended to my business. This bitch had me all types of fucked up.

She already didn't have Somalia, because she had been staying with Khanna since the accident along with Karizma and KJ. I'm sick and tired of dealing with the women that Khan choses to keep in his life. These bitches were going to put me into an early grave.

*****

I cancelled my family's Sunday dinner for the month. It just didn't feel right with so many holes in my family. Even though our dinner was cancelled that didn't stop everybody from still coming over and demanding I cook.

"Has anybody heard from Alani?" Khanna asked while bouncing Kadir on her leg.

"No, I haven't heard from her since Kay-Kay's party," I spoke solemnly.

La'La was my second daughter and I loved her more than just her role as Khan's baby mama. She had this aura about her that makes people just want to be in her space. Even though I hate how she just up and left, I somewhat understood.

Emotional pain eventually starts to weigh heavily on the body and she needed a break. I wish that she would have at least let someone know that she was okay. Instead, we are sitting here play the waiting game waiting for her to return.

Her daughter, Karizma, had been growing up so fast I wish she could see the milestones that she had been missing. I knew she would be fucked up if she knew that Khan was in a coma. She may act as if she didn't care, but even a fool can see the love she holds for my son in her eyes.

My cooking along with my thoughts were interrupted by a knock at the door. I answered it without checking who it was and was pleasantly surprised to see La'La.

I let out an excited squeal and embraced her, but something pushed me back. When I glanced down at her protruding belly my mouth dropped.

"I hope I'm not too late for dinner," La'La spoke.

"I ought to fuck you up and I would if it wasn't for this," I said rubbing her stomach.

"Let's eat so I can fill you in," she replied and I led the way to the kitchen.

"GlamMa, cake, cake" Karizma hugged my leg.

"Kay-Kay!"

Karizma hid behind my leg trying to shield herself from her mother. I noticed the solemn look her face, but she had to understand that her daughter hadn't seen her in months.

We retreated to the kitchen and she spilled it all. I had my cup ready to catch all the tea.

Chapter 52

Chino

"Somebody call some hoes up, I'm trying to get my dick wet," I laughed after throwing back a shot of Hennessy.

Being the boss man had its perks and I was loving it. I had bitches at my beck and call and I had turned the trap house into my own little bachelor pad.

"Yo, Khan and Rock don't like us shitting where we lay our heads, meaning no hoes where we got our work at," Mont said.

"Nigga, I don't give a fuck about none of that shit you talking. Khan put me in charge and told me to run things how I see fit. Shut your mouth talking to me; matter of fact, I'm docking your pay. Maybe that'll show you not be coming at me sideways."

That nigga looked pissed off, but I didn't give a fuck. I did what the fuck I wanted, when I wanted, and how I wanted. This was the life I'd dreamed of since I was a little kid. I had always wanted to run things alongside my big cousins. Niggas used to play me off to the side claiming I was too young. They always promised to put me on once I got older, but my mother decided she wanted to move away.

She claimed to have wanted a fresh start after my father and his best friend were gunned down in a "home invasion." Truth is I killed both those niggas then staged the homicide.

I came home from school one day with a fucked up ankle and a broken arm. I limped into the house only to find my sperm donor with his best friend bent over the edge of the couch pumping in and out of him.

The smell that permeated the air was enough to make me regurgitate the entire contents of my stomach. I backed out of the house and grabbed the gun that I had buried in the back yard that I had taken from Khan.

When I made it back inside and saw my "father" on his knees sucking dick I lost it. I aired both of their asses out; they never even knew what hit them. When the realization of what happened set in, I felt no remorse. I just knew I had to act fast. As disgusting as it was I redressed them both and ransacked the house. I cut myself using glass from the broken table, laid on the floor, and waited for my mother to get home.

When she did she was distraught, but I was there to help her through it all. What type of son would I be to let my mother go to bed each night with a booty bandit? After a while I guess living in the house she used to share with him became too hard to bear because she uprooted us and moved to North Carolina.

I hated living down there, but as soon as I got old enough, I moved right back. Now I was back living the life I was supposed to be living and I was going to bask in the ambiance of it all.

Chapter 53

Alani

Finding Khan in a coma caused mixed emotions to surge through my body. I didn't want to, but I allowed Megan to convince me to go see him. When I made it back to him, my heart beat out of my chest.

The only man I have ever loved was laid up looking like he was on his deathbed. Well, he could possibly be on his deathbed. I walked over and rubbed his dreads. They were freshly twisted and pulled back, but his face was swollen and he was wrapped in bandages.

I pulled up a chair beside his bed and cried into his chest. If I had lost him, I would have died; not physically, but it would have felt like it. We were on such bad terms and there we so many things left unsaid. If we wouldn't have been fighting so much maybe he would be okay. I wish I could just hold him tight and never let him go.

"I'm here now hoe, so you can dismiss yourself," Somaya said walking in.

"Hoe? Last time I checked you were sleeping with a man of mine not the other way around."

"Bitch well let me recheck that for you, the day that you abandoned your daughter on her birthday, yeah I know you remember that day, you thought it was cute to blast the fact that you slept with MY MAN earlier that day. Now like I said before, dismiss yourself."

I didn't even bother responding, I just gathered my things and walked out the room. I grabbed my daughter and walked out the house. She was kicking and screaming, but I didn't care. It was time for me to regain control of my life.

***

Karizma had been coming around and starting to recognize me more. For the first couple of days she screamed and cried asking for her "Mama." I consoled her as much as possible, now we're almost back like we never left.

My biggest regret in me leaving to get my head together, was leaving my daughter. Even though I felt my leaving was for the better, I didn't stop to think about how Karizma would react to it. I'm pretty sure Khan was raising my daughter in the same home as his baby mama, but I can't blame anyone but myself.

Being a parent is a full-time job that you don't get to clock out. I dropped the ball by uprooting and leaving the state.

Khan being in a coma had reminded me how much I still love him. My time away gave me time to reflect. Although I've been attempting to force myself to get over him, I have not been able to. So now I'm just embracing it, I'm in love with Khan and I think I always will be.

He was my first everything and even though he dogged me out every chance that he got, what we had was true love and true love doesn't just die. Our love was real and there was no changing that. I left Khan because I couldn't let him continue to think it was okay to fuck me over and get away with it. I left him to teach him a lesson, but I think we've both learned.

He has kids with Somaya now and I have a baby on the way with Rich. We can both co-parent with the parents of our children and rekindle our relationship. We were a force to be reckoned with in these streets and I don't see anything changing it.

***

I packed Karizma up and hopped in my car with Mama Megan's house set as my destination. I felt that maybe if Khan felt my presence or heard my voice it would wake him up. When I arrived, I was relieved to see his baby mama was gone.

I put Karizma in her room to play and made my way to Khan's room. I didn't want my daughter to see her father, hero, and protector in that state. When I made it inside Khan was sitting up in bed pulling the tube out of this throat.

I went over to assist him then grabbed a cup of water to soothe his throat. He just stared intently into my soul while drinking his water. His gaze was burning a hole in the side of my face, causing me to look down at the floor.

I have never in my entire life felt so insecure before. I looked up and just as I had guessed he was still staring at me. I walked over to him to touch his face but got the shock of a lifetime.

"Don't fucking touch me!"

"Khan, I was just coming here to check on you," I spoke back in a trembling voice.

"Like you checked on your fucking daughter while you were on your extended hiatus? Naw, I'm good on that. Send my mama up on your way out," he harshly spoke.

"I called you several times, you never answered the phone or returned any of my calls."

"You left and come back a liar?"

I had no more fight left in me, so I turned on my Giuseppes with my head hung low and walked out the door.

"Don't even think about taking Kay-Kay with you, she doesn't need your unfit ass!"

His last statement caused me to stop my stride and hit an about face.

"How dare you call me unfit, when Karizma didn't see you for the first part of her life? Who do you think took care of her then? When she was up crying all night running a fever, who the fuck do you think was there? It damn sure wasn't your bitch ass! If anything, Rich is a better father to her than your ass, so you can miss me with that bullshit. When you remember what type of bitch your baby mama is then you can hit me up to see your daughter. Until then, fuck you Khan!"

I turned around to walk out the door again only for my stride to be halted again. This time it was a bullet whizzing by my head. I turned around to face Khan with wide eyes. This nigga had really shot at me.

"Bitch, if you think you're about to walk out this house with my daughter you got another thing coming. Next time I won't miss."

"I'm not letting you or your slut ass baby mama raise my damn daughter Khan!"

"Bitch you don't have a choice. Now get the fuck out," he said putting the gun down on the end table.

I walked over to him and pushed his ass out the bed onto the floor. He had a cast on his leg still and Megan had already told me that he would need physical therapy in order to walk again.

I didn't say shit to his ass walking out of the room and the house. I decided to leave Karizma figuring I had gotten through to Khan. That nigga isn't stupid, I'll be back to get Kay-Kay tomorrow.

I meant what I said about not allowing Khan and his slut to raise my daughter like they are just one big happy family. If Khan won't agree to co-parenting and setting up a schedule for Kay-Kay to spend time with the both of us then he won't see her until he grew the fuck up. Either decision was fine with me.

Chapter 54

Rock

The doctors from the mental institution that I had Margo committed to called saying that she had made vast improvements and that they would recommend that she be discharged home. Nobody wants their baby mama sitting in the nut house so of course I allowed for her to be discharged.

When I went to pick her up, her face held a blank expression. I attempted to embrace her, but she just walked right past me to my car and got in. I already knew that was going to be a long day.

I didn't care how much the doctor's said she was better I didn't trust the bitch as far as I could throw her and I couldn't throw her so I didn't trust her. She damn sure wasn't going to be living under the same roof as me and my daughter.

I copped her a little two-bedroom rancher and got Khanna to decorate it for me. I will always take care of Margo, she birthed my seed. But we will never be anything more than co-parents. I couldn't trust her around my daughter and that's what was fucking with me the most.

"Where are we Josiah?" Margo asked. I guess the bitch had finally found her voice.

"Baby girl, you are home sweet home," I said putting the car in park before stepping out.

"This isn't our home Josiah and where is Josiana?" She asked me.

"Do you really think I'm going to jump and allow you to see my daughter, the very same daughter whose head you put a loaded gun to? Bitch be lucky your ass still breathing for pulling a stunt like that!" I snapped.

I had been trying to remain cool since I picked her up, but every time I looked her in her face all I could picture was her threatening Josiana's life.

"Josiah I was going through postpartum depression I've told you that already. I told you that I didn't even need to be in that place with all those crazy people."

"That wasn't for you to decide, now let's go inside so that you can see your new place because you won't be living with me Simple Sarah."

I didn't give a fuck about none of that shit Margo talking, she wouldn't be sharing a bed with me ever again.

***

I sat at the head of the table, a spot that is usually reserved for Khan, but I have to step up to the plate and run things in his absence.

"I called you all here because the big Homie is out of commission for the moment. I need all you niggas to step your game up because we don't have room for fuck ups. It's grind mode and if you niggas can't take the heat or the pressure you can bow out gracefully now. If you still down get the fuck out and go make this money!"

I got up from the table and went in the back to the office. Khan being out of commission had put all of our business in my hands. We had been making an attempt to dabble in legal business ventures, hence our reasoning in leaving Chino in charge of the illegal shit.

That forced my hand into going to an important business meeting alone. I washed my hands over my face feeling overwhelmed. The saying, 'heavy is the head that wears the crown' rings true, but they also say that God only gives his hardest battles to his strongest soldiers.

Chapter 55

Khan

After waking up from that coma if I had to compare the pain I was still in it would be like getting involved in a multicar pile up. My mouth was dry as shit, but I couldn't do anything with that tube down my throat. I went to pull it out just as Alani walked in. She helped me pull it out and gave me some water.

I guess she thought shit was cool trying to touch my face and shit. Alani up and leaving was the most disrespectful shit she could have done. To just leave her daughter's birthday party without as much as a word.

When she pushed me out the bed I would have fucked her up if it wasn't for the fact that I couldn't feel my legs and had a cast on both of them. Alani had been loyal to me and our cause over the years, but her turning her back on Karizma was something I couldn't forgive her for.

If she needed some time to herself, she should have said that and I would have given it to her. I would have paid for her to go on vacation or some shit. But no, Alani has to do shit her way, on her time. Only this time she will be paying the consequences of her actions.

She claims to have called me on numerous occasions, but I have no recollection of it.

I continued to lie on the floor in deep thought and pain for what felt like hours. Finally, my mother showed her face; I guess Alani's petty ass never told her to come upstairs.

"OH MY GOD KHAN!" she said rushing to my side. "How did you get down here?"

She helped me up off the floor and I responded, "La'La's dumb ass pushed me down here."

"What did you do to her?" she asked me with questioning eyes.

"Nothing, I just told her she wasn't seeing Kay-Kay with her unfit ass."

WHAP! A slap was delivered to the side of my face once I was back in bed.

"Boy, is you stupid or is you fucking stupid? Why the fuck would you tell her that? She has been nothing but good to your simple ass and you still find a way to shit on her. Even with y'all being divorced you still manage to fuck her over in the end. How dare you call her unfit when she was the only one taking care of a child that the both of you made together?

I swear Khan, you are your father's child. Neither one of you are the epitome of a good man. I don't care how mad you are at her you should never talk to the mother of your child that way. I'm done doing this same song and dance with you," my mother said then walked out my room.

I listening to everything that she said, but I wasn't trying to hear none of that shit.

***

Hood doctor come to check my vitals and instead of one of my loved ones telling me what was going on with me it was him to do it. Hood Doctor told me that I would need physical therapy if I ever wanted to walk again.

That car accident had me all fucked up. But the thing that had fucked my head up the most was the fact that I have yet to see my bitch. Somaya has not even attempted to bring her dirty ass over here.

I wanted to be back on my feet as soon as possible so I had my father call the best physical therapist in the area to come get me straight. My mother was mad at me and she wasn't talking to me; otherwise, I would have asked her. She flat out just wasn't fucking with me. I swear the women in my life are handful.

But in order to get a grip on my life as it spiraled out of control, I first had to get back on my feet, literally. All of my business ventures have been left in the hands of Rock. If it was anybody else, I would have been worried, but since it was Rock everything is all good. Rock had been my nigga since diapers so we both had each other's best interests at heart.

For that time being, I was just trying to spend time with my kids and focus on getting better. But when I got my hands on the mothers of my children I was definitely going to be applying pressure especially to Somaya's ass.

It seems like every time I try to stick it out and make it work with a bitch they shit on me. For her to not come to check on me in my time of need just shows me her character. This one incident alone shows me that the bitch I shared a bed with is not the woman I thought she was.

Chapter 56

Somaya

I stood up from the bathroom floor after praying to the porcelain Gods and wiped my mouth with the back of my hand. Instead of brushing my teeth, I gargled with a bottle of Jack Daniels. They say the best way to get over a hangover is to keep on drinking, so that was what I had planned on doing.

I was in a tremendous amount of pain after the car accident I got into with Khan. I haven't seen his ass since then. I know he's trying to keep my kids away from me. He hasn't even called to check up on me.

I grabbed my phone and called his mother. She shooed me away from her house the last time I went over there, but that day she was going to give me some answers.

"Megan, I know Khan is there with some bitches around my kids. Tell him to bring his ass home now!" I went in as soon as she answered the phone.

"Bitch, your drunk ass is slurring in the phone at eleven o'clock in the morning. Khan just woke up out of a fucking coma, so while I make sure my son is straight I suggest you come up with an excuse as to why you weren't the first face that he saw."

She just hung up on me and I had immediately sobered up. Damn, I had been so drunk since the car accident that I forgot that Khan ended up in a coma. Megan telling me that he was up made me jump up to clean our house. There were empty liquor bottles, cigarette butts, carry out trays, and trash throughout the house.

I got started cleaning only to be startled by someone walking into the house. I went to see who it was and it was Khan in a wheelchair being followed by Rock and Chino.

"Bitch get the fuck out of my house!" Khan's baritone voice boomed off the walls. I ignored his statement.

"Baby, you're awake. I was just getting the house in order for your arrival. Did you bring the kids?"

"Rock, get this bird brain ass hoe the fuck up out my house. Chino, call a maid service to come clean my crib, then call La'La over here," he shouted out demands.

"Khan, what's wrong?" I asked him.

"Do you think I would really bring my kids to a house that looks like this? You must have slipped and bumped your head on one of these Jack Daniels bottles. Now get the fuck out of my house."

I guess I wasn't moving fast enough for him because he spoke again.

"NOW SOMAYA!"

"You really think I'm about to leave and you just told your cousin to call your home wrecking ass baby mama over here?" I said to him with my arms crossed.

"La'La would have never let my house look this nasty. She would have been by my side the entire time I was out. She would have my children with her and she also wouldn't be drunk this early in the damn day. So while your dizzy ass is trying to talk down on my bitch you need to be getting some pointers from her. Don't worry I'll ask her if she's teaching any classes on how to be a down ass bitch!"

Other than the time Khan caught me drinking and smoking while I was pregnant he has never talked to me like that before. He has a way of making a person with the most confidence in the world feel small. I bowed my head and started walking towards the stairs.

"Naw bitch, I've bought everything that's in this house therefore you're not taking anything out of it. Be grateful that I'm letting you walk out if here with the clothes on your fucking back."

I just walked towards the door and sneakily grabbed my car keys off the hook near the door. He might think that I'm bowing out gracefully, but I got something for his ass.

***

I left the house that I shared with Khan and picked up all my kids. I lied to both Khanna and Megan telling them that Khan sent me to get them. I then went to the bank and withdrew all the money he had put in my bank account just in case he decided to be petty and freeze the account.

Once he caught whiff of me taking the kids I knew he would stop at nothing to get me to bring them back. I went and copped us a little spot near my old stomping grounds and furnished it with the help of some guys I knew.

Khan wasn't about to keep putting me out of a house he claimed was ours every time he got good and ready. He was famous for throwing hissy fits and kicking me out. Only he would try to keep the kids from me every time, even Somalia.

"Mommy where's daddy? Why are we here and not at home? I don't like it here. This house has roaches, Mommy I'm ready to go home," Somalia cried and complained.

"This is your home now Mali, so shut that shit up! Your daddy doesn't want us anymore!"

"I don't believe you! You're lying my daddy loves me," Somalia screamed then ran off to her room. It was a good thing she did because I was fixing to beat her ass.

I fed my twins and laid them down for a nap then cracked open my bottle of Jack. After the long day that I had, I needed that drink. After smoking a blunt and killing half of my bottle I ended up dosing off into a peaceful slumber.

Chapter 57

Khan

After getting my house in order, I got Chino to run me on a few errands. It was killing me from the inside out being immobile. This was something I probably could have never gotten used to.

After making sure my cash flow was straight I made my way to the most important stop I needed to make. I detested the fact that I sit in the car while he handled business for me. As time slowly ticked by, I was getting antsier by the second.

Finally, after what felt like forever Chino finally came out of the house carrying the twins in their car seats with a sleepy Somalia following behind him. Once he got them situated in the backseat he hopped in the driver's seat and took off towards my house.

I glanced back at my kids and my heart swelled with so much joy. Regardless of what I may go through with their mothers, I love my children to the moon and back. They are the only things in this world I know I've done right. I may be a no good dude in the eyes of a lot of people, but I strive to be a great father to all of my children.

"You did the right thing by calling me Mali."

I knew giving her a phone would work for my benefit. Somaya didn't even know that I had given her a phone.

Somaya knew what she was doing by trying to take my kids away from me. She can go wherever the hell she wants to, but my kids will be with me. She thought that she was slick, even though I'd told her on numerous occasions that there ain't nothing slick to a can of oil.

I saw her when she grabbed the car keys, but I allowed her to take them. I used to fuck the brains out of the bank teller so she notified me that Somaya cleared out our joint bank account. From there everything else was easy. I run the entire seven cities and the dudes that she got to help her move work for me.

I waited a while before making my way over there to get them. You would think that she would have decided to get her shit together, only that was not the case. Chino showed me the picture of her passed out drunk with a bottle of Jack Daniels in her hands was enough for me.

Once I got home and situated, I called Alani to come and help me out, only to find out she had changed her number. I had no choice but to call my sister over to help me out until I was back on my feet.

While waiting for Khanna to arrive, I sat and reflected on what had become my life. Somaya dumb ass had my house looking like a pig pen. She had just had my kids and all she wanted to do was drink like a fish. If Alani was still my bitch, if she wasn't there when I woke up, she would have been buck naked in the kitchen fixing me something to eat when I got home.

Somaya being drunk that early in the day was really distasteful. I should have left that hoe in the Portsmouth slums I found her in. I hated comparing her to my ex-wife, but it was hard considering Alani was everything Somaya wasn't.

Thinking about Alani had me feeling extremely bad about how I had talked to her. The only girl that had ever been down for me and I'd cussed her out and called her an unfit mother. I called my mother to see if Khanna had gotten there to get Karizma, but she told me Alani had come and got her.

My blood boiled and I wanted to get up to storm over there, but my legs prevented me from doing so. These women were going to be the death of me.

Chapter 58

Kane

It had been a few days since Khan woke up from his coma and went home. He didn't want it, but I had hired somebody along with a physical therapist to come and care for him until he was well. Khan wanted Alani to come nurse him back to health.

I had gotten all the kids with the exception of Karizma and brought them back home with me and Megan. Alani had come to get Karizma and refused to answer the phone for anybody before eventually changing her number on us.

She had even moved out of her townhouse so nobody knew where she lived. Since Megan had taken all of the grandkids out to the park and to get ice cream I had decided that I would go check on Khan.

When I arrived at his house I let myself in with Megan's key. As soon walked in, I walked right back out. About fifteen minutes passed before someone came to the door and I went back inside.

"I know this isn't the best way to meet somebody, but hi my name is Farrah and I'm Khan's physical therapist," the girl that answered the door spoke with her hand out for a shake.

I looked at her hand as if it was disease ridden before looking her up and down. She had on Khan's robe and it was slightly open revealing that she was naked underneath. Not that I didn't already know considering she was straddling Khan's wheelchair while riding him like she was starring in the Kentucky Derby.

"Bitch, you probably got my son's nut on your damn hand, I'm not touching that shit."

"Pops!" Khan said giving me a look that told me I needed to watch my tone. Not that I gave a fuck.

"I pay you a pretty penny to help my son get back on his feet. Not for you to be in here checking to see if his dick still works. If I needed somebody for that I would have just went down to the fucking strip club!" I snapped.

"Pops, you don't have to talk to her like that."

"Shut the fuck up Khan, your simple minded ass is always thinking with the wrong head. Then you turn around and fuck these thots giving them all this attention and taking up for them, only to wonder why they start acting a plum fool when they realize you ain't shit, but a dog ass nigga!"

"Oh you think your shit don't stink huh?" Khan said wheeling himself closer to me. "You think I don't know about the little bitch you left my mama for when I was a little jit. Judging by the way your jaw is touching the floor you didn't. I know all about how you left my mama to fend for herself and YOUR two kids while you traveled the world, building a family with another bitch. Look at the pot calling the kettle black, man get the fuck out my house with yo bullshit!"

"Nigga, you are going to respect me whether you want to or not. Even though I wasn't here physically, I was still here for you, your mother, and your sister. I'm the reason you are the man you are today!" I lashed back.

"You ain't nothing but another nigga that bust a million-dollar nut and made something better than himself! Get the fuck out my house! Farrah lock the door behind this nigga."

I looked at Khan before walking towards the door. I could do nothing but shake my head at the man he had become. He had become me and I could only blame it on myself.

Megan had done what she could in raising our kids; in fact, she did a phenomenal job, but at the end of the day I should have been there. A woman can't teach a boy how to be a man. It's hard for a boy to become a man getting fed only from a woman's hand.

I should have been there for my family to help build with them and guide them in the right direction. Maybe then our lives wouldn't have turned out so full of turmoil.

<u>Chapter 59</u>

<u>Rock</u>

I was dressed down in a Brooks Brother's Regent fit suit and tie with driving moccasins. I was looking good and smelling even better wearing Calvin Klein's Eternity cologne. I walked into the biggest building in the Virginia Beach Town Center with my briefcase in my hand and my confidence through the roof.

"I'm here for a meeting with Giovanni Milano," I spoke to the receptionist.

"He's been expecting you. I'll have someone escort you up."

I followed the burly Italian to the elevator to get upstairs. He escorted me to a room, told me to have a seat, then left. I checked out the room before sitting down, it was fully equipped. It had a full-sized wet bar, a table full of different breakfast foods and pastries, and the whole shebang. The floor to ceiling windows drew my attention, along with the breathtaking view of the city.

I sat down at the table waiting for Giovanni to make his arrival. I was getting antsy, in my mind I wanted nothing more than to get this show on the road. Half an hour had rolled by before Giovanni and some of his men walked into the room, laughing and smoking cigars like they hadn't kept me waiting. Before they could even sit down, I spoke up.

"Glad y'all could make it. But check this though, I'm all about my coins and my time is money. So if you don't mind I would like to get this show on the road."

"Who are you talking to nigger?!" one of Giovanni's minions said. I hopped up and pulled out my gun only for security to hold me down and pry it out of my hands.

"Everybody calm down, like my good friend Josiah here just said let's get this show on the road," Giovanni said taking a seat at the head of the table.

I straightened out my suit and gathered all of my papers out of my briefcase. Khan and I were trying to open a few restaurants, car washes, barbershops, beauty salons, and some more stuff. We both had the mind for business, although neither one of us had a degree. The meeting with Giovanni came into play, because we didn't want to step on anybody's toes and start an unnecessary beef.

He ran the cities from behind the scenes and we wanted to retire eventually. That was where we wanted to be in the upcoming years. Our current plug had been bullshiting us for some time, so all in all, we just wanted, no needed, to start a business relationship with him.

He could supply us with the drugs we needed to flood the streets while we washed our money through our legal ventures.

"So we're trying to take over the seven cities without stepping on any toes. This city is big enough for all of us to eat and coexist peacefully without any beef or wars starting. This is where we will be setting up more shops around town." I pulled out a map of where we would be opening different businesses and passed it around the table.

"You keep saying we, but you are the only one here, where is your partner?" Giovanni asked.

"He had a little accident and is recovering now, but I'm perfectly capable of handling this meeting on my own."

"If he can't even make it to this meeting how can we trust him?" The minion spoke again.

"I'm here on his behalf and that is all that matters, now back to business"

"So, if I agree to supply you and allow you to open up shop what is in it for me?" Giovanni asked.

"I'm not asking you for permission to open up shop I'm simply letting you know where I will be. Now as far as you supplying us this is where the real conversation will happen."

We had started to discuss numbers and I left out of the office a happy man. Thing was I couldn't forget the way his minion peered at me the entire time. He seemed as if he was mad at me, like I had pissed in his frosted flakes this morning.

I knew as my business continued with Giovanni I would have to watch out for him.

Chapter 60

Bam

I was sitting on Blake's lap in the trap house I ran counting money and wrapping it in rubber bands, showing my baby the ins and outs of what my days. He was going on tour soon and I had wanted to spend as much time with him as I possibly could.

I knew I was going to miss my baby as soon as he left me, so I had to soak up as much of his love as I possibly could to last me the length of time he was going to be gone.

As soon as we finished up the last of the count I turned halfway around to kiss his full lips. He hungrily sucked my bottom lip into his mouth returning the same amount of passion. He flipped me around and feasted on my neck while stripping me of my shirt, then wrapping his lips around my nipple in one swift motion.

"Ahh," I let out a slight moan relishing in the euphoric feeling he was giving me.

Blake switched to the other nipple showing it just as much attention as he showed the first. He was a skilled multi-tasker because he had unbuckled my pants and his fingers had made their way to my honey pot.

I started grinding on his finger while he tickled my G-spot. Just as I was about to reach my peak he pulled his fingers out and brought them to my lips and I licked each one.

I hated when he would take me to the brink of an orgasm then stopped, but he always made up for it in the end. I also loved how he could make me cum without ever sticking his penis in me.

Blake stood up with me in his arms and in a swift motion dropped his pants and was balls deep in me. I tried to stifle my moans so that nobody else in the house would hear me, but I just couldn't help it.

"AHH, FUCK! BEAT THIS PUSSY UP NIGGA!" I screamed out in ecstasy.

"Damn baby you got that shit dripping," Blake groaned my ear.

I didn't know how much more of him punishing my pussy I could take. The way he had my little ass up in the air only heightened my pleasure. The fact that he could drop me any minute just did something to me.

"Blake baby, I'm about to cum," I all but whispered as my eyes rolled to the back of my head and an orgasm took over me. My body convulsed and Blake came shortly after.

He slowly let me down and I grabbed some baby wipe out of my purse to clean us off.

"Baby, so I've been thinking. The more my career starts to take off the more I'll be traveling the world doing shows with Rich, the less I'll be home with you," Blake said then kissed my lips.

"And," I said waiting for him to get to the gist of this conversation.

"So I think we should have a baby so that you will have someone to remind you of me and to keep you company whenever I'm not around."

At first I couldn't even speak, I just looked up into his beautiful brown eyes. We had talked about having kids in the future, but I didn't know that the future would come so soon.

"I'm sorry baby, is it too soon?" Blake added once he didn't get a reaction from.

"No, boo it's fine I would love to have your baby!" I screamed before jumping into his arms.

"Now let's wrap our business up here so we can go home and get started on this baby," Blake said before slapping me on my ass making me giggle

Being with Blake made me feel like a little school girl. He made me feel all bubbly and fuzzy inside he gave me a feeling that I didn't even get from Rock. Sometimes it takes for you to deal with a nothing ass nigga to prepare you for the real man that's waiting for you.

Blake had showed me a love I'd never known existed and I never wanted that love to end.

***

So much had been going on in our lives that Alani and I didn't have much time to link up so we made it our business to get together at her new house to catch up. We were going to go out and have lunch, but neither one of us like being around too many people so her new house was the best choice.

I told her to call Envy and Khanna so we could all get together and catch up simultaneously. I grabbed the food I had picked up from wing stop and made my way to her front door. She moved out of the townhouse she shared with Rich and into a four bedroom, three and a half bathroom house in the same neighborhood as our mother.

Last time I talked to her, she said that she needed to get away from everything that reminded her of heartbreak and truthfully you couldn't blame her. She was dealt a hard hand in in life when it came down to love and she deserved happiness.

I knocked on her door and waited for her to answer. She opened the door and I got a huge shock. Her pregnant belly greeted me at the door first.

"Bitch when did this happen!?!" I squealed with delight. I placed the food a table in the foyer and rubbed her stomach.

"Girl, bring your ass in here I'm hungry as a hostage, but I might as well wait until the other girls get here so I can fill everybody in all at once."

I nodded my head in agreement and followed her into the kitchen.

"Where is Kay-Kay? God Mommy misses her chunky monkey."

"Girl, I finally decided to let my baby out of my sight, so she's with Megan. Megan has all of her grandkids so much you would think that they were her kids. I just missed her so much while I was gone that I just wanted to love on her. Kay-Kay had been around Somaya so much that she was calling her mama and I can't have that. Plus, Khan threatened to take my baby away from me by calling me an unfit mother, so I didn't want him to get any bright ideas."

"I know that I can't keep my daughter away from his family though or even him for that matter. I don't have any family outside of Ma so I think it's good that she gets to grow up receiving so much love."

Our mother was black balled by her family because she had gotten pregnant and decided to keep the baby, instead of getting an abortion. If she had gotten that abortion I wouldn't have had my best friend.

"I'm loving this new you so much! Envy and Khanna need to bring their slow butts on I'm ready for you to dish all this tea!" As soon as I said that in walked the two we've been waiting for.

We all exchanged greetings, fixed ourselves drinks and plates of food, before making our way to her "Woman Cave" as she calls it.

"Allow me to get this all out before y'all chew me a new asshole okay," Alani said and we nodded our heads before allowing her to continue.

"Okay so you all already know what went down with me and Rich. Well I've been in a constant mental battle with myself since then. I have been in love with Khan for as long as I can remember and Rich stepping out on me reminded me of that. It was just the reason I needed to leave him alone and go running full speed ahead back into the arms of the only man I love.

Khan has cried about how much he wants to get back together and in several weak moments that I have had we've slept together, even before Rich and I parted ways. Well the last time was on Kay-Kay's birthday. He came to drop the kids off including Somalia, sexed me so good he put me to sleep and when I woke up he was gone.

When I got to Mama Megan's house with all the kids I see Khan and Somaya all booed up like they are the happiest couple in the world. Somaya and I exchange words, but in the end I leave. At first I was just going to go home to get myself together, then come back for Kay-Kay, but Mrs. Fitz, the lawyer that handled my divorce, convinced me to hit Khan up and tell him that I needed some time away and that I would be back for Karizma. He never answered me, but I knew Karizma would be in good hands.

He kept claiming that he wanted to be with me, but when I decided to put my pride aside and give our relationship one last try he decides that he wants to make things work with his current flavor of the week.

Khan had successfully turned me into his side chick. I'm no better than Khan or Rich or even Brooke for that matter. I willingly fucked a man I knew was in a relationship and I cheated on the man I was in a relationship with. Not to mention I am once again pregnant by a man that has another woman pregnant at the same time. I don't know how I could continue to be so stupid over these men."

Once Alani finished pouring her feelings out to us we all sat there lost for words. Envy was the first to speak up.

"You can't keep beating yourself up about this. Shit happens in life that's what they made toilet paper for. You just have to learn how to pick yourself up and keep it pushing. You have another baby on the way now and you have to show this baby along with Karizma what a good mother is. Learn from your mistakes and teach Karizma how to be a lady. You're going to be alright."

We all got up and embraced a crying Alani. It's crazy how you can be so close to somebody and not know what they going through. I know how it is to face demons nobody knows about.

After all the water works were out of the way to laugh and joke around like we always did when we got together. We were just having good time.

Well we were just having a good time until I got a call that two of our traps had been robbed and burned to the ground.

Chapter 61

Khan

I've been slowly regaining the strength in my legs thanks to Farrah. I've been walking just a little bit, but only with the help of a cane. Farrah had to take a couple of days off to help her mother out. So she sent someone in her place to help me out. I know what y'all are thinking and no I'm not fucking her.

"Khan, are you hungry I just finished cooking your dinner," Karissa called out to me.

I eased my way up off the couch and made my way to the dining room to eat. Karissa had cooked me an Italian style feast and it was only me and her there.

"Damn girl, you didn't have to cook all of this shit, who gone eat it?" I asked her digging into the plate she made for me. "And who taught you how to cook like this?"

"I apologize, I'm just used to cooking big meals for my family. My mother taught me how to cook."

I didn't say anything else as I stuffed my face until I was interrupted by my ringing phone.

"I'll grab it for you," Karissa said hopping up from the table. She brought it to me and it was Rock.

"Talk to me," I spoke into the phone.

"My nigga somebody just took all the kids and burned the house down!" Rock spoke in code.

"On my way!" I said ending the call.

"Karissa, I need you to drive me somewhere."

"Okay, let me straighten up the kitchen first," she replied.

"Naw, we're leaving now!" I got up out the chair and moved towards the door as fast as my body would allow me to.

We hopped inside her car and drove to the trap. When I pulled up EMT's, police, firefighters, and my workers that hadn't been killed were all there. Bam, Alani, and them were all also in attendance.

Somebody had grown enough balls to take food out of my kids' mouths and try to stop my cash flow.

"Is this your new flavor of the week?" Alani asked.

"La'La, now you know this isn't the time nor the place for this shit." I massaged my temples.

That precise moment was not the time to be questioning me about where I chose to stick my dick. If memory served me correctly she divorced my ass.

"Your right, I'll be by your house later to discuss some things."

I didn't even bother responding to her.

"SOMEBODY GET ME SOME FUCKING ANSWERS! I DON'T GIVE A FUCK WHAT YOU HAVE TO DO! AINT NO WAY IN HELL TWO OF MY BIGGEST MONEY MAKING SPOTS GET TOUCHED IN ONE NIGHT AND NOBODY KNOWS SHIT!"

Everybody was standing around like my shit didn't just get touched. I couldn't care less about the fact the twelve was still there. I needed answers along with somebody's head on a silver platter.

"What the fuck happened here?"

I turned around and my pops was standing right behind me.

"The fuck you think happened my nigga," I countered. I was still tight with that nigga for the talking out the side of his neck to me at my crib.

"Lil nigga, I done told you to watch your fucking mouth when you are talking to me."

My jaw started to clench there was just too much shit going on all at one time. I needed to be finding out who burned my shit down to the ground after stealing my work, not getting locked up for beating my pop's ass.

Karissa grabbed my arm as I attempted to take a step towards Kane. I had to let this nigga know that there wasn't no bitch running through my blood. All of a sudden his attention was no longer focused on me. I turned my head to follow his gaze and he was staring straight at Karissa.

I stepped completely in front of her to block his view. For some strange reason I felt the need to protect her.

"Khan, who is he?" Karissa asked me.

"Nobody, lets go," I told her grabbing her arm only for her to snatch away.

Karissa walked towards Kane and touched his face while I stood there confused. This was looking like some crazy love connection type shit.

"You're alive." Karissa examined Kane's face like he would turn to dust at any minute.

"What the fuck is going on here?" I asked, my face etched with a look of bewilderment. They never responded to my inquiry.

"She told me you were dead," Karissa whispered.

"I'm going to kill that mother fucker!" Kane snapped snatching away from her. "Khan you better not have stuck your dick in her!" Kane added pushing me.

"Fuck wrong with you nigga! You gone stop putting your fucking hands on me, I can fuck whoever, whenever I want."

"Not her you stupid ass little boy, she's your fucking sister!"

My world stopped for moment and I just looked between the two of them. *What did this nigga just say?*

Chapter 62

Kane

When I pulled up to what used to be one of Khan's traps the last thing that was on my mind was that I would find the daughter I was told died during child birth along with her mother.

Karissa was the spitting image of her mother, she had some of my features and my rich dark skin complexion, but for the most part she looked just like Gianna. She only resembled Khanna and Khan a little bit.

Khan grabbed her and they hopped in her car and drove off. I continued to stand there with my feet glued to the same spot. If my daughter was alive then that meant her mother was alive.

And that was about to open a whole new can of worms. Giovanni Milano didn't forgive easily and even if he did, deflowering his only daughter was an unforgivable task.

Back then I owned a landscaping company, but Megan didn't know how deep I really was in with the Milano crime family. I fed her a lot of bullshit stories about what was really going on out in these streets. She was always stressing me about not being out in the streets because she didn't want to lose me to them.

If only she knew that I was knee deep in the game. I had built up a loyalty and a friendship with Giovanni and had become his right hand man. So he looked at me sleeping with his daughter as the ultimate betrayal.

Knowing that my daughter was still alive let me know that his daughter was still alive. Giovanni wasn't going to let that shit slide and I knew this was only the beginning of war.

*****

My phone was ringing which caused me to wake up out of my sleep. I glanced at the time and noticed that I had only been asleep for about three hours. I grabbed my phone and hit the ignore button.

After the previous night's events went to the bar and got drunk off my ass. I didn't want to completely forget about what happened, but I did want to temporarily get if off my mind.

Turning over, I wrapped my arms around Megan and attempted to go back to sleep. Whoever it was calling me wasn't letting up because my phone was ringing back to back relentlessly. I grabbed it and answered.

"Yo!"

"Daddy, can you come get me, I'm scared?"

I looked at the screen and didn't recognize the number, but it didn't sound like Khanna. That let me know that it couldn't be anybody other than Karissa. I sat up in bed now fully awake.

"What's wrong?"

"I told Nonno that I had come in contact with you and the other side of my family and he got one of his body guards to lock me in my room. They have been following me around everywhere I go keeping an eye on me. I tried to lose the tail he placed on me and when he found out he locked me in my room."

"Where are you I'm on my way?" I asked her.

"I'm texting you the address now, hurry daddy I'm petrified."

I ended the call and got out of bed. You would never know what Giovanni had up his sleeves. I didn't think he would do anything to Karissa, but in this life you can't put anything past anybody.

He would stop at no limits to get vengeance against me, for what he felt like was treason.

"Where are you creeping out to?" Megan asked sitting up in bed.

"I have some business to take care of I'll be back in a little bit," I told her kissing her lips.

"Mmmhmm, I hope for your sake that's true," she said, but I could tell that she knew there was more to the story. I was thankful that she didn't question me any further.

*****

I pulled up to the address that Karissa texted me and there was a gate surrounding the entire property. Just as I was thinking about how I was going to get in the gate opened. Everything about this felt like a setup, but for any of my offspring I would lay down and die.

I pulled around the spiral driveway and Bruno, the head of security was standing out front. I took a deep breath before exiting the car, but not before checking my glock to make sure it was fully loaded and I had an extra clip.

"Kane."

"Bruno."

"It's been a long time," Bruno said.

"Tell me about it."

"You know the deal, hand it over."

If he thought that I was going to go into the lion's den unarmed then he had another thing coming. Bruno ought to have known how I was by then, I know a lot of years had passed, but I'm still the same nigga.

"Bruno you already know that's not about to happen. Just look the other way, you remember when I helped you out with that little problem you had to make sure your wife didn't find out?"

Bruno had a thing for messing with younger girls. Only, one time shit blew up in his face. He had this seventeen-year-old girl in his little bachelor pad and her father tracked her phone to find out where she had been running off to.

He called the police and they bust up in the place. The girl cried rape and they were fixing to throw Bruno under the damn jail. That was until I killed all parties involved and removed all history from the police database.

"Good luck, Kane," Bruno said and walked around towards the back of the house.

I opened the double colonial style doors and walked inside with my gun hanging beside my leg. I walked up the stairs although I didn't know exactly where I was going.

I saw security walking down the hall so I crept into one of the bedrooms. I screwed on my silencer and peeked out the crack in the door. As soon as the security guard walked into my line of sight, I plastered his thoughts all over the wall.

He hit the floor with a thud which drew the attention of another guard. When he came my way his fate was the same as the other. Once I felt like the coast was clear I went in the direction they had just come from.

I walked into the room of the door that they were standing in front of and saw Karissa lying in bed sleeping. She was undeniably my child and I was couldn't contain the joy that I felt inside of me.

I was all messed up in the head when I was told that my wife and child died during child birth. Karissa was a piece of me and I hated the fact that I had live so much of my life without her. The void that had been placed in my life was now filled.

I shook her awake, pulled her hair back from out her face, and kissed her forehead.

"Baby girl, let me go make sure the coast is clear so we can head out. Grab whatever you want or need and I'll be right back."

I went to make sure nobody else was coming. When I didn't see anybody I went back inside to grab my daughter. I grabbed her duffle bag, threw it over my shoulder, then picked her up.

"Daddy you came to get me," Karissa said slightly slurring.

I don't know what Giovanni gave her, but it had her all loopy, and her eyes weren't dilating like they should have. I walked out the door and attempted to make my way down the stairs and out the door.

But before I could get there, shots rang out. I ducked down and pulled out my glock. I bust back in the direction the bullets came from and made a mad dash towards the front door. I was struck by a bullet in my back, but I continued out the door.

As soon as I made it outside with Karissa still in my arms I was struck over my head, which caused my knees to buckle and me to black out.

Chapter 63

Megan

Kane's sneaky dick ass thought it was cool for him to sneak out of my bed to go and do whatever it was that he had on his agenda. I played like I was sleep and listened to his conversation.

I couldn't hear what was being said on the other end, but I could tell that it was woman. If Kane thought that I was going to sit around and play the fool for his ass again, then he can cancel Christmas.

My heart has endured too much pain at his hands for me to ever go through that shit again. No wonder Khan had such problems with the women in his life. Look at who his father is and the shit that he has done.

I guess womanizing was passed down to my son genetically. It was just too much like wishful thinking for me to expect somebody to know better than to play with the feelings of a woman. Especially a man I raised and a man that I gave children to.

If Khan or Kane want to sleep around, then they should just tell the women they are with. I will dust off my crown and bow out gracefully if Kane wants to have other women.

I wasn't willing to share a man with anybody. If only he would just be honest with me that is all that I can ask for. Even though it would feel like he ripped my heart out of my chest and drove over it with a tractor trailer, it was something that I would respect.

I respect honesty and Kane is not being honest with me. When he does sneaky shit like he had been doing, I stopped trusting him.

Without trust we have nothing and Kane has completely used up all the trust that I have for him.

I didn't know if we could come back from the road we'd been traveling down, but only time could tell.

Chapter 64

Rock

Ripping and running around town to find out who had messed up my cash flow had tired me out. Even though I was mentally and physically exhausted I couldn't rest. It was hard trying to take care of my daughter while holding so much court in the streets, so against my better judgment I let Margo come back home.

I know what y'all are thinking, why would I welcome Simple Sarah back into my home, my life, and my daughter's life? But it really had seemed like she changed, plus I felt it was better than having a stranger around to take care of my daughter.

I walked inside of the restaurant Khan and I had just opened. Things were coming along nicely, and I was in awe of the turnout. The place was cleaned up and all the workers had returned home for the day. Opening day was a week away, so I knew we would be ready.

"Damn bro, you did your thing on this one." Khan complemented.

"Naw nigga, we did it."

Khan was like my brother; we are in this shit together.

"Alright let's get the fuck out of here, it's time to pound the pavement for some answers."

Just as we were about to make our way towards the door to lock up we heard something coming from the back. Khan and I looked at each other before simultaneously pulling out our straps.

Before we could even start towards the back, out came Giovanni Milano.

"This place has come along beautifully figlio," Giovanni said in his thick Italian accent.

"What the fuck are you doing in my place of business?" Khan asked taking a step forward. I reached out my arm to pull him back.

"Your family has posed treason upon mine and now it is time to pay up for past mistakes."

"What are you talking about?" I asked him confused.

"Karissa, my grand-daughter, is your sister Khan."

"Tell me something I don't know."

"You father fucked my young daughter and got her pregnant. Kane was a good friend of mine and he betrayed me by touching the one thing I held near and dear to my heart."

"What does that have to do with us? You obviously knew that before you decided to supply us."

"Well I thought I could get over it, but seeing as how this black mother fucker looks just like his father, I decided I would bring you to your knees instead. Starting off by making your supply dry up, giving somebody else the chance to come in and take over."

"Fuck you bitch nigga, we'll find somebody else to supply us!" Khan snapped.

"We'll see," Giovani said.

He turned to walk out and one of his goons shot the place up with a semi-automatic weapon causing dirt and debris to fly everywhere.

Whenever we think we are getting things under control everything goes from sugar to shit.

Chapter 65

Khanna

After a long, tough battle the courts awarded Dae'Sean full custody of Kadir. To say I was devastated would be an understatement. I cried the entire way from the courthouse. The tears clouded my vision so much that Alani had to drive for me with her very pregnant belly. She tried to console me, but there wasn't much she could do unless she could get Kadir back for me.

I then knew what it felt like to lose a child, Kadir is still living and breathing, but it didn't mean a thing if I couldn't wake up to his chubby cheeks every day.

Dae'Sean still didn't even have KJ, but he wanted to take my son away from me. I had to go home to an empty house and drink myself to sleep. I sent all the other kids I had been watching to my mother's house, because I was in no condition to be caring for them. Alani offered to stay with me, but I just wanted to be alone to drown my sorrows in a bottle of Jack Daniels.

Dae'Sean did a damn good job as deeming me an unfit mother. Because I was technically unemployed and have no verifiable income other than the money my brother and now my father laced my bank account with every week, they awarded Dae'Sean and I joint custody. But Dae'Sean had physical custody.

I broke down in the courtroom while they tried to pry Kadir from my arms. I held on as long as I could, but I didn't want hurt him so I eventually let go. But I fucked up the courtroom on my way out.

I couldn't see my son without permission. If Dae'Sean said no then I wasn't able to see Kadir. Kadir was the only person in this would that gave me unconditional love. Without my son by my side I saw no reason to live.

Which led me to downing every pill I could find in my house and washing them down with Jack Daniels. I glanced at the mirror and mascara ran down my cheeks. I punched the mirror in frustration causing it to shatter.

I climbed in the tub I had filled with hot water, but not before getting my bottle. I continued to drink until I passed out. If I couldn't have Kadir with me at all times then maybe we could be together in my dreams.

Chapter 66

Alani

My belly had been growing at an alarming rate. At my last doctor's appointment, I insisted my doctor check to make sure there was only one baby in there. I was ordered a strict bed rest, but I couldn't sleep knowing my family was at risk.

I had been pounding the pavement, busting niggas upside their heads, alongside Bam, to find out who robbed and set the traps ablaze.

Once night fell, Bam pulled up like clockwork and I hopped in the stolen car.

We road out in silence while Bam puffed on a blunt. The only thing that could be heard was the sounds of J. Cole's track *Tale of Two Cities*. We pulled up on our destination.

Bam checked her gun to make sure it was locked and loaded before hopping out the car. I stayed inside waiting for her to be finished, while watching her back. I didn't want anybody to see my belly fruit and look at me as an easy target so I just played the cut.

"Bitch run that shit!" Some random little nigga ran up on me and said. He even put a gun to my head.

I threw my hands up in surrender. "I don't have much, but what I do have is in the middle console. You can reach in and get it. Just please don't hurt me, I'm pregnant."

"Hoe you must think I'm stupid or slow, you grab that shit and give it to me. I want all of it too!"

Natavia Presents

I reached in the middle console and handed him the money I had stashed in there and instead of leaving he stood there thumbing through it.

"What's all that shit you was just popping, you little pussy ass nigga?" I asked him. I had grabbed him by the collar of his shirt and practically pulled him through the window. I placed my gun to his temple and he started shaking.

"My bad shorty, you can have your money back," he said with his voice trembling.

"Naw, I don't want it back, but you were just the nigga I was looking for let's take a ride. You must not know who the fuck I am."

"Oh shit! I didn't know that was you La'La. I would have never tried to do no shit like this."

I didn't even answer him.

By this time Bam had made her way back out of the house we were parked in front. She hopped in the backseat and I got out and put the young bull in the backseat with Bam then hopped in the driver's side.

I drove to a nearby Denny's and we all got out. We took a seat in the back and when the waitress came we all placed our orders. My child had me hungry as a hostage, but I decided to get down to the business at hand.

"What do y'all want? I'm sorry for trying to rob you. I didn't know you was the wife to the King of the City."

"Ex-wife," I clarified.

"Please don't kill me. I got a daughter to feed."

"Shut the fuck up. If we wanted to kill you, you would have been dead already. We want to know who burned down our trap houses. You scratch our back we scratch yours. Your daughter will never want for anything, and you can retire from your job as a stick up kid."

"I'll tell you everything you want to know." He said before giving everything to us straight with no chaser.

By the time he was finished my mouth was touching the table and I had been rendered speechless. This revelation was a complete game changer, but I had come up with the perfect plan.

Chapter 67

Khan

I was sitting on the edge of the bed with wetness drenching my face. My chest was tight and I could barely breathe. I gripped the piece of paper I was holding and re-read it again for what seemed like the hundredth time. I felt like if I continued to read it, the words that decorated it would somehow change.

But clear as day the piece of paper that cast a black cloud over my life read:

In the case of Khan Junior

Khan Thomas is not the father.

I wish I had never gotten him tested. I could have lived my life never knowing the truth. When KJ was a baby he looked just like me. But as he got older his looks changed, and he started to look more like Brooke.

The papers from the DNA testing center also stated how they were backed up which is what took so long for me to receive the results. As if I didn't have enough shit going on in my life, I just had to be hit with this.

Farrah came into the room and took a seat beside me. She started to rub my back, but I really just wanted to be left alone. She didn't know my pain, so she couldn't comfort me. There was only one person that could.

Farrah dropped down to her knees and unleashed the beast from his resting place. She took my limp dick in her mouth, but he wouldn't budge.

"Khan I just want to make you feel better and take your pain away."

"Well you can start by getting your shit so I can drop your simple ass off home," I responded.

She sighed in frustration, but removed herself from the floor and did as I requested.

Once she got all of the shit she had lingering around my house together I assisted her with carrying it all to my car. I cranked the car up, turned the radio up, and drove off into the night. I didn't want her to try to spark a conversation up, so I drowned out any conversation she could have attempted.

When I got to Farrah's house I didn't even bother helping her get her shit out of my car. As soon as she closed my trunk I drove off, not caring whether she got into the house safe or not.

I drove to the address I had stored into my memory bank and parked down the street once I made it. I walked the short distance it took for me to get there from where I parked and let myself in by breaking a window. I knew she wasn't home because her favorite car was still parked in the driveway.

I grabbed a bottle of Hennessy out of the stash I knew she would have and made my way to her bedroom. It was my favorite so she continued to buy it out of habit.

I rolled up a blunt, sparked it up, and took shots while waiting for her to arrive.

Chapter 68

Margo

Being back home with my man and daughter felt great. While I was away I resented Rock for putting me in a nut house and keeping me away from my daughter, but every time I looked into his sexy ass face I forgave him a little bit more.

I was never going to hurt my princess, I just needed to get Rock's attention. If it didn't have anything to do with Josiana or the streets Rock wasn't paying me any mind. Of course now I realize the flaws in my behavior.

My family was complete and I couldn't have been happier. I never had the chance to know what a real family felt like, therefore it was something I wanted for my daughter.

My father had been absentee my entire life. If I went to visit him, it would seem as if everything was good. He would give me money, take me shopping, we would go on daddy daughter dates and the whole nine. When I went back home to my mother I wouldn't hear from him.

Eventually I just stopped calling him and going to visit with him. Me calling him was the only way we would talk anyways. That was not a life I wanted for my princess.

I was so happy when Rock told me I could come home to the both of them, I twerked the entire time I was packing my clothes. Now, the only thing left for me to do was to plot my revenge.

Rock's little gutter rat is going to pay for trying to tear apart my family. I feel bad that her baby died, because I don't know what I would do if something happened to a child that I carried for nine months, but now it was time for her to move the fuck on.

Nothing will ever come between my family and I. I had Rock's only child and I planned to keep it that way. I would not be sharing baby daddies with anybody; especially a ratchet chick like her.

Bam trying to kill me and Rock while I was pregnant is something that I will never be able to forgive her for. For the time being, I was just enjoying being wrapped up in Rock's strong arms again, while I sat back and plotted my revenge.

Chapter 69

Alani

Bam dropped me off at my house and as soon as I stepped out of the car an eerie feeling washed over me. I pulled out my gun as I made my way inside my house. Once I cleared the first floor I made my way upstairs.

There was a noise coming from my bedroom so that was my next stop. I pushed the door open and someone was coming out of the bathroom walking past the door.

I put my gun up to their head about to pull the trigger until they turned around.

"Khan, what the fuck are you doing in my house? You scared the shit out of me!"

He just collapsed down to his knees and hugged my legs. I put my gun up and rubbed his back and his head simultaneously. His head was buried in my stomach, but not hard enough to hurt me.

"What's wrong Khan?" I asked him sincerely.

"He's not mine La," was all he said.

I already knew what he was talking about, so I just continued to hold him while he let it all out. Khan has always been the head of his family. Ever since he was younger he has had to work to provide and make sure everybody else is straight.

Khan is the epitome of a strong man.

I helped Khan off the floor and sat him down on the bed. I started towards the bathroom to run him a bath and clean him up, but he pulled me back to him. He lifted my shirt and kissed my belly.

I allowed him to remove all of my clothing one by one. When I was fully naked, he just stared at me. I started to feel self-conscious and insecure under his gaze.

It had been so long since he had seen me fully nude and I had gotten a whole lot bigger.

"Stop that shit! You have always been the most beautiful girl in the world to me," he said pulling me back to him.

This was so wrong with me being pregnant with Rich's baby, but it felt so right. Khan laid me down on the bed gently then stood to remove his clothes. The way he was chiseled and cut up was as if the gods had hand sculpted him.

Khan towered over me and kissed my lips gently. Then he trailed down the length of my body; his lips leaving behind dampness on my skin. My body quivered under his touch reacting in ways only he was able to uncover.

When his lips reached my honey pot he kissed both of my inner thighs before diving in.

"Ahh," I let out a soft moan before gripping the back of his head.

Khan helped me explore my body so he knew how to make me reach different heights of pleasure. He continued to slurp and lick driving my body wild. He moved his head just as my pussy squirted out.

Khan dove back in and made me cum so many times I lost count. My clit was sensitive to the touch, so I tried to crawl backwards on the bed. Khan was not allowing it. He wrapped his arms around my lower body and continued feasting on my kitty.

"Bae, I can't take it anymore," I moaned out breathlessly. "I'm cumming again!" I screamed out. I came again and this time he stopped.

I lifted my head from its resting position and looked down at him. The moonlight that shone in the room illuminated his face and I saw it glistening from my juices running down his cheeks.

Khan wiped his face with his discarded shirt then climbed up the bed. He kissed my lips at the same time he slid his rod inside of me.

"Ahh, fuck La'La! This shit tight and wet as shit."

Instead of fucking like we usually so, Khan moved at a steady pace making love to every inch and crevice of my body. The only sounds that filled the room were our pants and the sloshing and slapping sounds from our intense love making session.

"Baby, I'm about to cum," I said in his ear while fucking him back.

"Did I tell you to come yet?"

"I can't hold it."

"You better, don't cum yet Alani."

"I'm cumingggggg," I screamed as an orgasm took over my body. I started shaking as a smile spread across my face. I had been so horny; being pregnant had my hormones in overdrive. I didn't have a man to take care of my needs so I had been taking care of myself. But you know what they say, there is nothing like the real thing.

"I'm going to make you pay for that," Khan said flipping me over before ramming his dick back inside of me.

I arched my back as much as my stomach would allow and prepared to take all that he was giving to me.

"Right there baby," I screamed throwing my ass back into him. His dick was so big I felt like he was rearranging my insides.

"Khan, I'm cumming again."

"I'm right behind you this time baby girl," he said right before he let his kids loose inside of me.

I collapsed on the bed and he rolled off of me. Khan pulled me into his arms and I went to sleep with a smile on my face happy and content. For once everything felt so right, and all I thought was here we go again.

***

I woke up early the next morning bright-eyed and bushy-tailed. I wanted to make Khan breakfast, but I knew I didn't have much food in the house. I kissed his lips before getting out of bed and quickly making my way to the bathroom to handle my hygiene.

I hoped he at least slept until I got back. He probably would the way he was snoring. After showering, I threw on a sundress, grabbed my purse, my shades, and my keys before leaving out the door.

When I got to the grocery store I quickly grabbed all of the things I would need before heading to the register. While I was standing in line, I saw the same person I had been seeing all over the store.

I didn't pay them much attention, if they wanted to be on good bullshit I wouldn't hesitate to put a bullet in their skull ending their very existence.

After checking out I loaded my car and headed back home.

***

When I pulled up there was a car I had never seen before blocking my driveway and someone sitting on my porch. I hopped out with my gun drawn pissed that I would have to move again, but grateful that Karizma was with her Glam-ma as Megan calls it.

When I got close enough to see who it was I lowered my gun.

"Goddamn Rich! I almost killed your ass. What are you doing here?" The words felt like déjà vu leaving my mouth.

"Why do I have to find out from tabloids and private investigators that I have a baby on the way?" He said showing me pictures in his phone. They were of me while I was in the grocery store. *I knew somebody was following me* I thought.

"Because, I'm not sharing yet another baby daddy with yet another bitch. Now you got your answer so get the fuck off my lawn."

"I'm not going anywhere so you might as well open this door so we can go inside and talk. Daddy's home now."

I was not about to open that door knowing Khan was somewhere on the other side.

"La'La, don't fucking play with me I'll kick this bitch in!" He snapped when he saw I wasn't budging.

"What the fuck you doing out here making all this noise, when you could be in here making me breakfast butt ass naked ready to take this dick again." Khan said stepping onto the porch. He hadn't stepped out far enough to see Rich yet, but shit was about to get real.

Chapter 70

Rich

"You fucking this nigga while you pregnant with my seed? Letting this bitch ass nigga nut all over my baby's head?" I asked incredulously.

"Rich just go I'll talk to you later," Alani said attempting to push me towards my car.

"Naw, bitch we ain't got shit to talk about. I should have known you wasn't nothing but a hoe. Just know I'll be back for custody of my baby. There isn't any sense in even trying to fight me for it. I'll win any day over a washed up drug dealer's ex-wife."

I started towards my car, but was hit over my head. I touched the spot where I was hit and felt blood. I turned around to see that La'La had pistol whipped me. Next thing I know I'm getting jumped by her and Khan.

Well that was until gunshots rang out.

I heard La'La scream and I hopped up off of the ground to protect her. Everything I had just said to her was out of pure anger. Truth is I was still in love with that girl.

Whoever was shooting was targeting this house purposely, because the middle-class bougie neighborhood La'La lived in wouldn't have regular drive-bys.

When the smoke cleared, La'La was laying on top of Khan bleeding profusely. His body was riddled with bullets. I rolled her off of him and her body was covered with so much blood I couldn't tell where she was hit.

I knew she was still alive because of the slight rise and fall of her chest, although it seemed like each breath could possibly be her last.

Khan on the other hand wasn't moving at all. Before I could check his pulse to see if he had checked out or not, the police, ambulance, and fire trucks pulled up.

I was tackled to the ground then taken downtown before even finding out if the mother of my child had a chance at making it.

Natavia Presents is now accepting submissions:

Natavia Presents is owned and operated by bestselling author Natavia of; "Who Wants that Perfect Love Story Anyway," "A Bittersweet Hood Dilemma," A Beauty to his Beast," and much, much more, also a subdivision of Shan Presents under the #Newprint network.

Natavia Presents is currently accepting submissions from new and experienced authors. If you are interested in getting your work published and in the hands of many of readers, please contact Natavia today.

Genres accepted are Urban Fiction, African American Romance, Interracial Romance, Street Lit, Paranormal Fiction.

Please send in the first 3 chapters of your manuscript, synopsis, and contact information to natavia.stewart@yahoo.com.